# The Home Stretch

# The Home Stretch

Dale Evans Rogers

with Floyd Thatcher

**WORD BOOKS**
PUBLISHER
WACO, TEXAS

A DIVISION OF
WORD, INCORPORATED

THE HOME STRETCH

Unless otherwise indicated, Scripture quotations are from the King James Version of the Bible. Other Scripture quotations are from the following sources:

*The New Testament in the Language of Today* (Beck) by William F. Beck. Copyright © 1963 by Concordia Publishing House.

*The Bible: An American Translation* (AAT) by J. M. Powis Smith and Edgar Goodspeed. Copyright © 1935 by the University of Chicago.

The Jerusalem Bible (JB), copyright © 1966 by Darton, Longman & Todd, Ltd. and Doubleday and Company, Inc. Used by permission of the publisher.

*A New Translation of the Bible* (Moffatt) by James Moffatt. Copyright © 1954 by James Moffatt.

The New American Standard Bible (NASB), © The Lockman Foundation 1960, 1962, 1963, 1968, 1971, 1972, 1973, 1975, 1977.

The New English Bible (NEB), © the Delegates of The Oxford University Press and the Syndics of The Cambridge University Press, 1961, 1970. Reprinted by permission.

The New International Version of the Bible (NIV), copyright © 1978 by the New York International Bible Society. Used by permission of Zondervan Bible Publishers.

The New King James Version (NKJV). Copyright © 1979, 1980, 1982, Thomas Nelson, Inc., Publishers.

The New Testament in Modern English (Phillips) by J. B. Phillips, published by the Macmillan Company, © 1958, 1960, 1972 by J. B. Phillips.

The Four Gospels (Rieu) translated by E. V. Rieu. Copyright © 1953 by Penguin Press, Ltd.

The Revised Standard Version of the Bible (RSV), copyrighted 1946, 1952, © 1971, 1973 by the Division of Christian Education of the National Council of the Churches of Christ in the U.S.A., and used by permission.

Today's English Version of the Bible (TEV), copyright © American Bible Society 1966, 1971, 1976. Used by permission.

ISBN 0-8499-3134-7 (pbk.)

*Printed in the United States of America*

89 80 1 2 3 9 BKC 9 8 7 6 5 4 3 2 1

# Contents

# Contents

# The Home Stretch

*Have you ever wondered why some people seem old at forty while others are young at seventy? I have. And as I've thought about it, I have come to believe that the secret is found in a rather obscure Old Testament verse. In a completely different setting and under circumstances we have difficulty imagining, the people of Israel heard these words from Moses' lips in one of his final speeches before his death, "I have set before you life and death, . . . therefore choose life" (Deut. 30:19, RSV).*

"The straight part of a race track from the last turn to the finish line."

The dictionary definition of *the home stretch* has a rather sterile and lifeless sound. But if you are sitting in the middle of an expectant crowd in the stands at a race track when a field of horses rounds that last turn, excitement reaches a fever pitch as their strides lengthen for the dash to the finish line. These are electric moments! Rider and horse appear molded together as one, both straining forward and giving it all they've got in anticipation of those last yards.

# The Home Stretch

## A Time to "Strain Ahead"

It is this mood and excitement that caused the apostle Paul to come alive when he wrote to his friends in Philippi, "I have not yet won, but I am still running, trying to capture the prize for which Christ Jesus captured me. I can assure you my brothers, I am far from thinking that I have already won. All I can say is that I forget the past and *I strain ahead for what is still to come;* I am racing for the finish" (Phil. 3:12–14, JB, italics mine).

Since Paul was writing from Rome, he knew his vivid imagery of a race would appeal to his Greek readers in the Roman colony of Philippi. Depending on the reader, one of two scenes would certainly come to mind when they read Paul's words: a runner lengthening his pace for the final sprint down the straightaway or a chariot driver straining forward with death-defying intensity as he grips the reins of his plunging horses—a scene straight out of the movie *Ben Hur.*

## A Time for Renewal

The imagery Paul used here and in various other places in his letters has always appealed to me. I've often been accused of living life as if it were a race. B.C.—before Christ in my life—I moved down the fast track in my drive for fame and what I thought then was success in show business. And then on that Sunday evening so long ago, when Dr. Jack MacArthur gave the invitation to accept the Lord, I raced down the aisle of that First Baptist Church of Eagle Rock and found peace and joy in the prayer room as I came clean with God and turned my life over to him.

My mother used to say, "Frances [my real name] always rushes into things. She is so impulsive!" I suppose she was right—especially since the day I committed my life to the Lord. But life is so full and the excitement of being a Christian is so great that pulling out all the stops and going full speed just comes naturally for me. This is why it is easy for me to identify with the race image that is so often applied to life and that Paul referred to in his letter to the Philippians.

For several years now, I have wanted to reflect on and write about that part of our lives we might call the home stretch. None of us knows just how long that home stretch will be after we've made it into and through what we now call midlife—a chronological range between age forty and the early sixties. Except for living wisely and carefully, there may not be much we can do about the length of the home stretch, but we can exercise a great deal of control over its quality.

And now that I can claim the distinction of being on the other side of the traditional three score and ten, I believe I've earned the right to have some opinions about the home stretch, although—Lord willing—I'm still a long way from the finish line.

Of one thing you can be sure: we're not going on a nostalgia binge. I refuse to sound like a senior citizen or an "older" person or someone in the "golden years." To me, those terms and the others that are in vogue have a negative, "over-the-hill" sound. I suppose "late adulthood," used by psychologist and social scientist Daniel Levenson, is the least objectionable to me.

At any rate, I identify with Bernard Baruch, a statesman and financier who died at the age of ninety-five, when he said, "To me, old age is always fifteen years older than I am." And I would add to that, "A person's true age is to be found in the years ahead, not in those already passed."

## An Adventure of Faith

But all of us, whether we're in our twenties, our forties, our sixties, or our seventies, are moving steadily toward the straight part of life's track that leads to the finish line. Each and every stage of life is part of the race. And for us Christians, it is terribly important that every inch of the straightaways and turns be a living adventure of faith irrespective of our immediate surroundings or circumstances.

# The Home Stretch

## *A Time for Excitement and Victory*

When the apostle Paul wrote that he was straining
for what was still to come and that he was racing
for the finish, he was apparently in prison in Rome.
He was most likely still suffering from an irritating
disability described earlier as a "thorn in the flesh."
Undoubtedly, the ravages of four shipwrecks,
thousands of miles of rugged overland travel on foot,
and physical beatings had left deep physical and
emotional scars. And while we don't know for sure,
Paul was in all probability between fifty and fifty-
five years of age—still midlife by our standards today
but late adulthood in the first century.

Yet there's no sound of pessimism in Paul's writing,
and he certainly isn't complaining about "getting old."
Quite the opposite—he's straining ahead and looking
forward eagerly. We get a picture of a man who is
alive every minute, enjoying the present and
anticipating the future.

In a keynote commencement address at
Pepperdine University in Malibu, California, Norman
Cousins (former editor of *Saturday Review* and
author of *Anatomy of an Illness*) made this incisive
comment to the graduating students in the Graduate
School of Education and Psychology: "The great
tragedy of life is not death but what dies inside of
us while we live."

He is so right! But then I'd add, "The great tragedy

of life is that so many Christians, instead of going into a sprint on the home stretch, seem to lose their zest for life and begin to coast. They look back instead of ahead and begin to sound like 'old folks.' "

## Eternal Life Has Already Begun

For the Christian, eternal life has already begun. And I believe that, short of an unexplainable debilitating illness, God intends for us to be full of life and busy for him.

I like the way the *Jerusalem Bible* speaks of Abraham's death: "The number of years Abraham lived was a hundred and seventy-five. Then Abraham breathed his last, dying at a ripe old age, an old man who *had lived his full span of years*" (Gen. 25:7–8, italics mine). I have the same feeling about Abraham that I have about the apostle Paul—he was always straining ahead and racing for the finish. In my dreams, I've had mental pictures of both Abraham and Paul. I've imagined them in all sorts of situations. But I've never visualized them relaxing in a rocking chair.

## Moses, an Old Testament Model

Have you ever wondered why some people seem old at forty while others are young at seventy? I have.

And as I've thought about it, I have come to believe
that the secret is found in a rather obscure Old
Testament verse. In a completely different setting and
under circumstances we have difficulty imagining,
the people of Israel heard these words from Moses'
lips in one of his final speeches to them before his
death: "I have set before you life and death, . . .
therefore *choose* life" (Deut. 30:19, RSV, italics mine).

Moses seems to be telling them that the choice
for *life* was theirs. They could decide whether or
not to live—to be really *alive.* And I believe Moses
knew what he was talking about. He was older than
most of us who are reading this book when he led
more than a million of his fellow Hebrews out of
Egypt into the unknown of the Sinai Peninsula.
Moses had *chosen* to live. And he had gone on for
forty more years to live a vigorous life under the
most difficult of circumstances. In fact, the writer
of Deuteronomy wrote this epitaph, "Moses was a
hundred and twenty years old when he died; his eye
was not dim, nor his natural force abated" (34:7,
RSV). This is why Moses is one of my real-life heroes.

## From Socrates to Bob Hope

From Moses, my mind wanders down through the
years to others who stand out because of their
accomplishments on the home stretch. Socrates
learned to play a musical instrument in his old age.

# The Home Stretch

Cato, the Roman soldier, statesman, and writer, learned Greek when he was eighty.

Michelangelo did some of his finest work as an artist when he was ninety. Verdi composed *Ave Maria* when he was eighty-five. Tennyson wrote "Crossing the Bar" when he was eighty, and comedian George Burns won an Oscar when he was eighty. Then there's Mother Teresa and Bob Hope, who have accomplished so much on the home stretch.

## Two Special Examples

But two names especially stand tall in my mind. First, there is the prize-winning author, James Michener, who wrote *Hawaii, The Source, Texas,* and many other bestsellers. Several years ago, at the age of seventy-five, he said, "I can hardly wait to get out of bed in the morning. I have so many exciting things I want to do." Mr. Michener has chosen life, and it is obvious that he has deliberately set out to live his full span of years.

The other person who stands tall in my life and memory is Mrs. Charles E. Cowman, who with her husband was a pioneer missionary to Japan and China in the early 1900s. In 1917, because of Mr. Cowman's ill health, they returned to the United States, where he died.

In 1925, at the age of fifty-five, Mrs. Cowman's first book, *Streams in the Desert,* was published and has now sold well over two million copies. Then, at age seventy-nine, she published a daily devotional book for young people entitled *Mountain Trailways for Youth*. When she was eighty-two, her *Traveling Toward Sunrise* was published and became a top seller in the devotional marketplace. Mrs. Cowman awakened a new person every morning, and she epitomized the words she had written earlier in life, "Unlike the flesh, the spirit does not decay with the years. We can keep on living abundantly and creatively until we die, no matter at what age."

This great Christian, whose words have touched millions of lives, died at the age of ninety. There was a parallel between her life and a story she once told: "Somewhere near the snowy summit of the Alps there is an inscription that marks the last resting place of an Alpine guide. Just three short words tell the story, 'He died climbing.' We often hear it said that a certain person is 'growing old.' But we don't grow old. We only *get* old when we cease to grow and climb."

## Living with an Expectant View of the Future

There seems to be a common cord that binds together the experiences and stories of all of these people I've just mentioned. They lived life with an expectant view of the future. From their point of view, they were never finished. There had to be a tomorrow because there were so many exciting things they wanted to do.

This idea was well expressed by Dr. Viktor Frankl, psychiatrist and survivor of a World War II Nazi concentration camp. Throughout his prison experience, he observed the reactions of his fellow sufferers, and somewhere he made this comment: "Survivors were people who believed they were unfinished with life." And in one of his important books, he built on this idea when he wrote, "It is a peculiarity of man that he can only live by looking into the future."[1]

Somewhere I picked up this little poem. I'm not sure who wrote it, but it ties in perfectly with what Dr. Frankl has written:

> Age is a quality of mind—
> If you have left your dreams behind,
> If hope is lost,
> If you no longer look ahead,
> If your ambitions' fires are dead—
>     Then you are old.

## *We Choose Our Future*

For me, the picture is beginning to come into focus. Late adulthood—the home stretch—is nothing more than the extension of a race that started with that first smack on the bottom and the first cry. Each day, each week, each year, and each decade build toward the home stretch. And what we are then is the result of the attitudes and dreams and hopes that we hugged to ourselves during our younger days. Dr. Paul Tournier, that much-beloved Christian psychiatrist from Geneva, understood this so well when he wrote, "In order to make a success of old age, one must begin it earlier."[2] In other words, our success in the home stretch is determined by the way we lived during our twenties, our forties, and our sixties.

At each stage of life, *we choose* what the next will be like. We decide whether tomorrow is flooded with sunshine or beclouded with oppressive storms, whether to change and grow or to remain static and get stale. It is *our* decision to be optimistic, to dream, to have hope, to live on tiptoe.

But even as I write these words, I want you to know that, of course, God's ways are not our ways. No matter how we choose or dream or hope, we will experience wrenching hard times, intense disappointments, and the ravages of grief. But even then, we choose our method and style of coping.

No, I'm not a Pollyanna thinker. But I have come to learn that our wonderful heavenly Father created us in his image. And as his redeemed sons and daughters, we possess the capability to think and act and live so that *every* part of our race is well run, especially that most exciting and potentially productive part of all—the home stretch.

## *Grow a Little Each Year*

Few writers have blessed the American scene more than nineteenth-century poet Henry Wadsworth Longfellow, who gave us such masterful works as *Evangeline, The Song of Hiawatha,* and *Tales of a Wayside Inn.* In the midst of all of his successes, though, were two great sorrows—First, the ill-timed death of his young wife in Holland and then, years later, the loss of his second wife, who was fatally burned in an accident at home.

Apparently, not long before Longfellow's death at age seventy-five, an admirer asked him how he continued to write so beautifully and remain so vigorous. Longfellow responded by pointing to an apple tree that was a riot of colorful bloom and said, "That is a very old apple tree, but the blossoms this year seem more beautiful than ever before. That old tree grows a little new wood each year, and I suppose it is out of the new wood that these blossoms come. *Like the apple tree, I try to grow a little new wood each year."*

I believe Mr. Longfellow had discovered a very simple yet profound truth. Life comes out of "new wood"—new growth. But the analogy shifts a bit when we move from apple trees to people. God, through the awesome and magnificent forces of nature, acts to produce "new wood" in the apple tree. But growth in the human realm is a deliberate choice of people. We *decide* to keep growing throughout our lives. When that decision is made, there are certain specific things we can do to enhance that growth process. And God has built into us the capability of doing those things that can and will contribute to our success in the home stretch.

But age is not a factor. Maggie Kuhn of the Gray Panthers understood this when she said, "Old age is not chronology. It's self-image and state of mind."

Maggie Kuhn's view of age was certainly shared by Mr. Hokusai, a talented Japanese artist, who at age seventy-five wrote, "From the age of six, I had a mania for drawing. . . . By the time I was fifty, I had published an infinity of designs; but all I produced before seventy is not worth taking into account. At seventy-three I learned a little about the real structure of nature, of animals, plants, birds, fishes. In consequence, when I am eighty, I shall have made still more progress; at ninety I shall penetrate the mystery of things; when I am one hundred, I shall certainly have reached a marvelous stage; and when I am one hundred and ten, everything I do, be it but a dot, will be alive."[3]

Physical energy may indeed diminish on the home stretch, but the Lord has given us another energy that is far more important and effective. It is this that we want to look at in the rest of our visit together.

# The Energizing
# Power of a
# Positive Attitude

*We aren't "grasshoppers" in a world piled high with giant difficulties. But if we allow our minds to become polluted by negative attitudes—if we think defeat—we lose sight of our possibilities in Jesus Christ.*

One of the most powerful sources of energy the good Lord has blessed us with does not come in a medicine bottle and cannot be administered with a shot. In terms of dollars and cents, it isn't expensive, yet it is a vital ingredient of life at every stage— especially as we move toward the home stretch. This great energy source has more than once changed the course of history, as both leaders and ordinary people have asserted *a positive attitude.*

There are those in some circles today who label this idea as superficial or phony. But I don't believe that for a minute. In fact, I've discovered that only a tough-minded person has what it takes to develop and maintain a healthy and inspiring positive attitude. Then, too, I've known some folks who seem to have the ridiculous idea that a positive attitude toward this life isn't realistic, that anyone who can see the least bit of good in what's going on in our world has his or her head buried in the sand. But nothing could be further from the truth!

## *Who Is in Charge?*

So often, we look at life through smeared glasses and allow our thoughts to be gloomy and negative. We act as if Satan was in charge instead of God—concentrating on the problems and the evil in the world instead of on the possibilities and the good. Like Peter, who was invited by the Lord one night to join him in a stroll on the waters of the Sea of Galilee, we take our eyes off of Jesus, look at the waves beating against our feet and legs, and begin to sink because our thoughts are negative and filled with fear.

Unfortunately, this sort of thing has been going on since the earliest days of our religious history. There is a fascinating story in the thirteenth chapter of Numbers that illustrates so graphically our tendency toward negative attitudes.

## *"Grasshopper" Attitudes*

First, though, we need to set the stage for the story. The time is roughly 1300 B.C., and the setting is Egypt, where the Hebrew people have been in slavery for about four hundred years. The characters are Moses and the Egyptian pharaoh.

Moses had been separated from his countrymen in Egypt for many years, but now he was back after his dramatic meeting with God at the burning bush near Mount Sinai. It was there Moses had received his commission to return to Egypt as God's messenger to the king, and it was there he had been told that he would lead his people to freedom.

The story of the spiritual tug-of-war between Moses and the great Egyptian pharaoh (Exod. 5–12:36) is a combination of suspense and high drama. Interspersed in the action were the nine plagues God sent as convincers that the Hebrews should be released. But the impasse continued until the firstborn in every Egyptian home was struck by the angel of death. Only then did Pharaoh give them permission to leave Egypt.

About two million Hebrews made a hasty exit with Moses as their leader. But they hadn't been traveling long before Pharaoh regretted his decision and dispatched an army to round them up and bring them back.

The Hebrews by this time had reached the edge of the Red Sea. Ahead was an impassable body of water, and behind was the pursuing army of Pharaoh. It was a real Catch-22 situation, but God told Moses to stretch his arm and staff out over the water. The master storyteller of the book of Exodus left us a vivid picture: "Then Moses stretched out his hand over the sea, and all that night the Lord drove the sea back with a strong east wind and turned it into dry land. The waters were divided, and the Israelites went through the sea on dry ground, with a wall of water on their right and on their left" (Exod. 14:21–22, NIV).

The second act of that drama was played out with the Egyptian army down in the bed of the Red Sea pursuing the Israelites. When the last of the Israelites had scrambled to high ground on the other side, the Lord told Moses to stretch out his hand over the sea again. And when he did, the waters rolled back into place with a roar, and the entire Egyptian army was drowned.

We don't have a day-by-day journal of what happened after that, but we do know that God led that undisciplined and noisy mob of about two million people on into the Sinai wilderness. From there they turned north to the wilderness of Paran until they reached the area of Kadesh-barnea, some forty to fifty miles south of Beersheba on the border of Canaan.

Through all of this trip from Egypt, however long it took and by whatever route they traveled, the Hebrews had been led, provided for, and delivered by God. Imagine! From the moment they had walked on the dry bed of the Red Sea with the water stacked high on either side, God had taken care of them. And he had continued to care for them throughout every mile of the trip. They saw one "miracle" after another.

That's the setting—now for the story. God told Moses to select one man from each of the twelve tribes of Israel and send these men north to reconnoiter Canaan. Each one of the twelve were leaders and chiefs—men of responsibility. They were commissioned to scout out the country, observe the people and the fortifications, and check out the crops and food resources.

We're told they went as far north as Hebron, about twenty or so miles south of the city we know of as Jerusalem in what would someday be Judea. The twelve men scouted the area for forty days and then returned to where the Israelites were camped. They were loaded down with produce and fruit— pomegranates and figs are mentioned. The writer who described the event even said, "They lopped off a vine branch with a cluster of grapes, which two of them carried away on a pole" (Num. 13:23, JB). Imagine, the cluster of grapes was so big that it took two men to carry it!

Then, after admitting that Canaan was a land that flowed "with milk and honey," the men went on to paint a black picture of doom and gloom. They reported that the people were powerful—stronger than they were. And they said, "The country we went to reconnoiter is a country that *devours* its inhabitants. Every man we saw there was of enormous size. Yes, and *we saw giants . . . We felt like grasshoppers"* (Num. 13:32–33, JB, italics mine).

## A Positive View

Two of the returning scouts had a positive and optimistic attitude. They urged their countrymen to march and conquer. Caleb, one of the two, said, "We are well able to do it" (Num. 13:31, JB). The other ten, though, filed the majority report, "We are not able to march against this people; they are stronger than we are" (v. 31). The majority opinion prevailed, and the feeling ran so strong against the two positive thinkers that "the entire community was talking of stoning them." It was only the intervention of the Lord that saved them from death (Num. 14:10–12, JB).

With our 20/20 hindsight vision, it is easy for us to be critical of those unbelieving and negative-thinking Israelites. And yet, over thirty-five hundred years later, our attitudes so often are much like theirs. We see ourselves as "grasshoppers" in a world of "giants." And this is true even though we have the advantage of seeing God at work throughout all intervening history, including perhaps the greatest miracle of all—the life, death, and resurrection of Jesus Christ.

As paradoxical as it may seem, the way of the Cross is the way of positive attitudes, for the Resurrection followed the Cross. It was on that first

## The Energizing Power of a Positive Attitude

Easter morning that life's negatives were turned into positives; and since then, people of all times have been able to see the world through a different set of lenses.

It is God's will, I believe, for us to have a healthy, hope-filled, and positive attitude toward life, even in the troubled times that plague our world. It is true that so much of today's news is bad. We are bombarded with bad news on six o'clock television and radio. Terrorism seems to have the upper hand; brothers are killing brothers in the Middle East; the world's superpowers specialize in name calling; and the threat of a nuclear accident or war hovers over us like a black cloud. And while all of this is going on, economic patterns are shifting so that there's a restless feeling of uncertainty even in the midst of apparent growth and prosperity.

But the fact remains that we aren't "grasshoppers" in a world piled high with giant difficulties; we are the redeemed children of a good and mighty God. But if we allow our minds to become polluted by negative attitudes—if we think defeat—we lose sight of our possibilities in Jesus Christ.


### *No Guarantee of Utopia*

Now, this isn't to suggest for a moment that I have fallen for the subtle heresy that has filtered into certain elements in the church and is creating confusion in the minds of many Christians. I'm referring to the idea that being a Christian guarantees success and prosperity—that if we have positive attitudes, give a certain percentage of our income to the church, and attend services every time the church door is open, our economic wants will be cared for and we can expect a trouble-free life.

God's grace isn't a payoff for good behavior. It isn't something we've earned or deserve. But it is ours in Christ, and it is adequate for our hard times as well as for our good times. Eugene O'Neill, in a moment of rare insight, seemed to capture this truth in a flash of inspiration when he wrote, "Man is born broken. He lives by mending. And the grace of God is the glue."

The apostle Paul knew all about this. In his letter to the Corinthian Christians, he mentioned his struggle with his "thorn in the flesh," which I mentioned in the previous chapter. He prayed three times that God would heal him. But the Lord simply answered, "My grace is sufficient" (2 Cor. 12:8–9). Then, as I read the next few verses, Paul's attitude shifted—"Most gladly therefore will I rather glory in my infirmities" (v. 9)—and he viewed his future with a positive and hopeful attitude.

## The Choice Is Ours

It is a sobering thought to realize that *we choose our attitudes*. Thousands of years before the development of modern psychology, the psalmist understood the workings of our human condition when he wrote, "For as he thinks within himself, so he is" (Prov. 23:7, NASB). Or to put it another way, "We become what we think about all the time." Our attitudes are controlled by our thoughts. We decide whether to be positive people who are fun to be with or negative people whom everyone wants to avoid.

One of the most exciting ideas that has come to me is that God wants us to move into every new day with a positive attitude of hope and expectation. He wants us to *make it* at every stage of our lives, but especially during our home-stretch years. God is for us! As Christians, we are to be positive witnesses of the Good News that Jesus Christ has set us free from negatives.

## *What Is Our Part in the Drama?*

Even though this isn't a "how to" book, I want to be very practical now. Since I believe it is God's will for us to have a positive, upbeat, and hopeful attitude toward life, and since I also believe that having positive attitudes is a deliberate choice we make, just how do we develop and expand this important gift? And it is a gift—one that God has already given us and is anxious for us to accept. But to accept that gift and put it into practice, I

believe we need to accept another of God's gifts—
perhaps one of the rarest. I'm referring to the gift
of *knowing how to see.*

Knowing *how to see the world around us* is an
important facet of this gift, for our world is perhaps
one of God's strongest arguments in favor of our
having a positive and hopeful outlook on life. The
psalmist understood this when he wrote, "The
heavens proclaim God's splendour, the sky speaks
of his handiwork" (Ps. 19:1, Moffatt). And Elizabeth
Barrett Browning caught a glimpse of God's creative
wonder when she wrote, "Earth is crammed with
heaven, and every common bush afire with God."

Earth crammed with heaven! I just don't believe
it is either normal or possible for anyone to think
negatively while looking out at sunrise across the
high desert where we live in California, or while
standing at sunset on the south rim of the Grand
Canyon. It is awesome to see the wonder of God's
hands at work during autumn in the Northeast, as
green leaves change to a vivid splash of red and
gold. And each spring in my native Texas, God's
hand moves across the plains and hill country as
bluebonnets and Indian paintbrush form a blue and
red carpet in the open fields and along the highways.

To really *see* the wonders of God's world around
us is a life-changing experience. For it is then that
we participate in the divine harmony that is to be
found in an intimate relationship with him.

But there's another side to the gift of knowing

how to see, a side that is a powerful force in developing positive attitudes. We must come to know *how to see ourselves as sons and daughters of God.* What an exalted place we have in God's creation! Way back in the earliest verses of the Bible, we read, "And God said, Let us make man in our image, after our likeness" (Gen 1:26). Then the sacred writer added, "So God created man in his *own* image, in the image of God created he him; male and female created he them" (v. 27).

## Our Heritage in God

Those electrifying words are very specific and to the point. We are made in God's image and are in a world of his making. It is true that the entrance of sin into the world sorely disrupted God's intention for his creation. But the great Good News of our Christian faith is that the life, death, and resurrection of Jesus restored once and for all God's order for all who accept him as Lord.

I somehow suspect that Ralph Waldo Emerson, the perceptive nineteenth-century American poet and essayist, understood what this means when he wrote, "What lies behind us, and what lies before us, are small matters compared to what lies within us." And it is what lies *within* us in Christ that has the power to turn our *every* negative into a positive.

If we rightly claim who and what we are as

## The Energizing Power of a Positive Attitude

Christians, our thoughts and attitudes are aligned with God—he is within us, and all of life becomes a positive expression of his love at work in us.

For me, one of the most awesome descriptions of what God intends us to be is found in the eighth Psalm. Evidently, the psalmist had experienced some moving moments as he looked up at the brilliance of a clear nighttime sky ablaze with stars and then reflected on his own insignificance in comparison. And then he goes on,

> Yet thou hast made him [man] little less than God,
>    and dost crown him with glory and honor.
> Thou hast given him dominion over the works of thy
>    hands;
>    *thou hast put all things under his feet."*
>                              Ps. 8:5–6, RSV, italics mine

Imagine! God intends for us, as people made in his image, to be in charge, to exercise mastery over his creation.

How is that possible? The answer, I believe, was given us by the beloved disciple of Jesus at the very beginning of his Gospel, when he made this startling statement: "But as many as received him, *to them gave he power* to become the sons of God" (John 1:12, italics mine). In other words, as we apply this promise to our thinking here—we have the power to think and act positively at every stage of life, including every yard down the home stretch, even during those hard and difficult times.

If there ever was a person who exercised the power and ability to think and act positively during the hard times of life, it was my great hero of the faith—the apostle Paul. We take our comforts and freedom for granted as we zip down interstate highways in automobiles that do everything but steer themselves. And those of us in the Western world are so accustomed to expressing and living our faith freely that we can't even begin to imagine what it would be like to be persecuted physically because we're Christians.

But Paul gives us a pretty colorful picture as we read what his Christianity cost him:

> I realize I'm boasting recklessly, but I have worked harder, been beaten countless times, been jailed frequently, and often faced death. The Jews beat me five times within one lash of the forty-lash limit. Three times I was beaten with sticks, once I was stoned, three times I was shipwrecked, once I spent twenty-four hours drifting in the open sea. I have made innumerable trips and been threatened by storms, by thieves, by fellow Jews, and by non-Jews. I have been in danger in cities, in deserts, on the sea, and often from impostors. I have worked at the task when I was exhausted, in great hardship, during sleepless nights, without food, exposed to the cold without enough clothing.[1]

Now, that is what I would call a vivid description of trouble and hard times. But right in the middle of that kind of life, Paul gave us one of the most earth-shaking promises in all of the Bible: "I can do all things through Christ which strengtheneth me" (Phil. 4:13). Another translation words it this way: "I can do everything through him who gives me strength" (NIV).

Even though Paul wrote those words while he was in prison, probably in Rome, he doesn't sound like a victim or like someone whose attitude has gone sour. He was a positive thinker even in jail because he knew who and what he was in Christ.

## To Be a Chicken or an Eagle

Recently, while reading the little book by my friend Dr. Norman Vincent Peale entitled *You Can If You Think You Can,* I was reminded of the old story of the confused young eagle who grew up thinking he was a chicken. According to the story, a boy, whose father owned a chicken farm, was climbing to the peak of a nearby mountain one day and discovered an eagle's nest. Removing an egg from the nest, he carefully carried it down the mountain. When he got home, he put the egg into a nest with some chicken eggs that were being tended by an old hen.

Some time later, all of the eggs hatched, and the little eagle grew up with his brother and sister chicks.

## The Energizing Power of a Positive Attitude

For a time, everything appeared normal; the little fellow seemed to think and act like a chicken. But one day while he was out in the chicken yard pecking away at the grain, he heard a scream. And looking up, he saw an eagle soaring high above in the wind currents. Something stirred down deep inside. An unexplainable urge impelled the little eagle to spread his unused wings. Even though he had never flown before, he sensed what to do and awkwardly flew a few yards. Then, with a bit more assurance, he flew a mile or so, and from there, he soared to the mountain peak that had been his first home. He discovered who he really was and never again pecked at corn in the chicken yard.

## *We're Shaped by Our Thoughts*

What people think is the inner force that shapes what they are and do. A hundred or so years after the apostle Paul's death, Marcus Aurelius, the Roman emperor who was also a philosopher, made this wise observation: "The soul becomes dyed with the color of its thoughts." And the wisdom writer in the Old Testament knew all about that when he wrote, "What he thinks is what he really is" (Prov. 23:7, TEV).

Happily, there are some things that don't change with the passing of time. Truth doesn't. Compare these late twentieth-century words with those of Marcus Aurelius and the Old Testament writer:

## The Energizing Power of a Positive Attitude

- "One prepares for old age [the home stretch] by taking a positive attitude throughout one's life."
- "My basic rule for health, energy, and long life is to keep your thoughts healthy and positive in nature."
- "The way you think about life can influence your lifespan and your health."

These twentieth-century writers and thinkers are right in tune with the rhythm of the past.

### The Home-Stretch Adventure

The home stretch of our lives is intended to be satisfying, rich, and productive. Above all, it is a time that calls for flexibility and an openness to change. But even beyond that, it is meant, I believe, to be the time of our greatest influence for good and for God. Contrary to what frequently happens, late adulthood is not a time for looking back, for living in the past. It isn't a time for grousing about the so-called "good old days." Instead, it is a time to approach each new day with excitement and anticipation.

Many years ago, noted American thinker and writer William James said, "Believe that life is worth living, and your belief will help create the fact." For the Christian, life is not only worth living; it is worth living to the fullest—positively and with exuberant optimism.

There are two great affirmations that are life changing. If daily we will fill these wonderful minds God has given us with these words, our attitudes and lives in every stage—but especially in our home-stretch years—will be filled with hope and meaning. Repeat them in the morning on awakening, in a moment of quiet at noon, and just before drifting off to sleep at night:

> This is the day the LORD has made;
>   let us rejoice and be glad in it.
> > Ps. 118:24, NIV

> But this I call to mind,
>   and I have hope:
> That the gracious deeds of the Lord
>   never cease,
>     his compassion never fails;
> They are fresh every morning;
>   great is his faithfulness.
> > Lam. 3:21–23, AAT

# Enthusiasm—
# The Art of
# Being Alive

*I believe that anyone who has the overflowing life of Christ in them is enthusiastic and really enjoys life! And when we enjoy life, it shows—it moves out with a powerful energy that those around us can feel. It is attractive and winsome. We get a lift when we're around people that enjoy life; we're influenced by them. They make a difference in our lives.*

"None are so old as those who have outlived enthusiasm." Although he died at the age of forty-four, Henry David Thoreau had learned early that enthusiasm is one of the most important ingredients of a rich, full, and useful life.

Enthusiasm—excitement about life—is important at every stage. But in the home stretch—those mature years of middle and late adulthood—enthusiasm is indispensable if we are to be the kind of people who are comfortable and at ease with ourselves. At the same time, enthusiasm is also absolutely essential if we are to be the kind of people those around us like and enjoy being with. Let's face it—limp, gloomy, and apathetic people are not especially pleasant to be around.

## Enthusiasm—The Art of Being Alive

We've all had acquaintances, I'm sure, who instead of "accentuating the positive" concentrate on the negatives—the kind of folks who look at a rosebush and see the aphids or the black spot instead of the roses. It is this kind of person who instead of being awake and sensitive to the beauty of an opportunity can only see the problems.

### *To Be Awake Is to Be Alive*

In *Walden,* Thoreau seems to relate being "awake" to that enthusiastic quality of life that he feels is important when he writes, "To be awake is to be alive." Then, a little further on, he explains what he means: "We must learn to reawaken and keep ourselves awake, not by mechanical aids, but by an infinite expectation of the dawn." I like that, for I firmly believe that as we Christians "live in expectation of the dawn," we will be awake and enthusiastic every moment of our lives—even in the midst of hard times and in our home-stretch years.

This quality of life is expressed vividly in a stirring book by Paul Horgan entitled *Lamy of Santa Fe.* With unusual flair, the author in this gripping biography describes the personhood and vitality of Juan Bautista Lamy, the first Catholic archbishop of Santa Fe.

Born in France in 1814, Lamy arrived in Cincinnati, Ohio, in 1835 as a young priest of twenty-five. Then, in 1851, he moved south and west to his "Desert Diocese"—the brawling and sprawling Southwest, consisting of northern Mexico and what is now Arizona and New Mexico. It was rugged and parched country, and only the hardiest of pioneers were able to survive. But for years, Lamy moved relentlessly across the arid and treacherous terrain of the raw frontier, ministering to the physical and spiritual needs of a people lacerated by the struggle for bare existence. His life was hard, and his experiences were often heartrending. But through it all, he maintained a spirit of high adventure that is colorfully portrayed in this descriptive comment of Horgan's: "He always awoke a young man."

What a wonderful way to express the enthusiasm, vitality, and zest for life that is meant to be ours as Christians! Being awake and alive—awaking every morning a new person—smacks of that kind of enthusiasm that energized Jesus' disciples when they finally understood that he had conquered death and the grave and was very much alive.

Actually, the drama and the miracle of that first Easter morning revolutionized all of creation. And that was seen dramatically in the changed lives of Jesus' disciples. Where three days before they had been paralyzed with fear and had gone into hiding, now they moved out into the open with seeming reckless abandon in their enthusiasm—their Spirit-intoxication. They were men *truly alive*. Fear and anxiety were forgotten; and after being empowered by the Holy Spirit at Pentecost, they moved out boldly beyond the narrow borders of Jerusalem and Judea "to the very ends of the earth" as they knew it. Theirs was a contagious faith.

## *Fullness of Joy—A Way of Life*

Enthusiasm, a welling up of excitement, an expectation of the dawn—that is precisely what God wants for each one of us. This comes through loud and clear in so much of Scripture. The psalmist put it this way: "In thy presence is fulness of joy" (Ps. 16:11). And the words of Nehemiah are just as apropos for us now as when they were first spoken to the Jewish audience: "The joy of the Lord is your strength" (Neh. 8:10).

What a marvelous definition of enthusiasm— fullness of joy. But this joy is not the same kind of giddy, surface "happiness" that we feel when things are running smoothly and going our way. Let's face it, things don't always work out the way we plan or hope for. There's much that happens to us that hurts. But the joy both the psalmist and the author of Nehemiah wrote about is more than a feeling or an emotion. Rather, it is a way of life in which our confidence in God is so strong that we are "full of joy" even in our most difficult times.

## An Enthusiastic Response

Moving over into the New Testament, we find a graphic picture of enthusiasm in Luke's description of the dramatic encounter between Peter and John with the crippled beggar at the Beautiful Gate of the Temple. Luke writes that after Peter had spoken the electric words, "In the name of Jesus Christ of Nazareth, *walk!*" the healed man "sprang to his feet, stood, and then walked." Then Luke continues, "He walked about, leaping and thanking God. Everyone noticed him . . . and recognised him . . . and they were all overcome with wonder and sheer astonishment" (Acts 3:7–10, Phillips).

The crippled stranger at the temple gate met two enthusiastic disciples of the risen Jesus, and he came alive with such fire and enthusiasm that everybody around got turned on. This same thing happened later when Paul and Silas began to witness for the Lord in the Greek seacoast city of Thessalonica. They hadn't been there long until it was said of them, "These men who have turned the world upside down have come here also" (Acts 17:6, RSV).

It is rather interesting to note that the word that is translated here as "turned" comes from a root word that means "to excite." Paul and Silas were enthusiastic witnesses for Christ who created excitement among their listeners. This is the authentic Christian lifestyle.

## *The Christian Style*

Now, this kind of a mood among Christians of any age was not meant to go out of style in the first century. It is our model today whether we're bucking bumper-to-bumper traffic on Franklin D. Roosevelt Drive along the East River in New York City or on Michigan Avenue in Chicago. It is the truly Christian style in the midwestern folksiness of Muncie, Indiana, and along the seemingly endless ribbon of concrete known as Interstate 10, that winds past colorful towns in West Texas. And it is also our model on the world's longest parking lot—the San Bernardino Freeway as it converges into the interchange in downtown Los Angeles.

But so often, even among Christians, I've heard it said, "How do you expect me to be enthusiastic in a world full of bad news? I get depressed every time I read the newspapers—even the comic strips are full of tension and stress. And as for the six o'clock news on television, all we get is a depressing litany of terrorism, nuclear threats, the arms race, and name calling. I just can't see any way out of this mess, and there certainly isn't much to get excited about."

## *An Affair of the Will*

It may not be easy—and frequently it isn't—but if a spirit of enthusiasm is the mark of an alive

Christian, there must be a way. And I think C. S. Lewis, with his customary perceptiveness, points the way in a comment he made about love: "Christian Love, either towards God or towards man, is an affair of the will."[1] The same principle applies equally well, I believe, to enthusiasm and being "alive": *it is indeed an affair of the will.* Nobody is enthusiastic by accident. It is something *we* decide to be and a style of life *we* decide to live.

Bruce Larson, gifted author and pastor, tells an utterly delightful story about a lady in the Seattle area who is eighty-four years old and is active in a number of worthwhile causes. She had been driving the same car for nineteen years. And evidently she had said at one time that when the old car stopped running, she would just give up and die. (It sounds to me as if she hated to buy a new car about as badly as I do.)

But one day the old engine finally belched black smoke and gave up for good. As the woman surveyed the lifeless car, though, she changed her mind and bought a secondhand, reconditioned engine. Now the nineteen-year-old car is still running—and so is she. This is what she told a *Seattle Times* reporter:

> As the cells in my body renew
> And my purpose in life I review,
> I find, growing older,
> I'm now growing bolder
> And increasingly hard to subdue.[2]

## Enthusiasm—The Art of Being Alive

That lady had enthusiasm for life, and she wasn't about to quit or be subdued, even at age eighty-four!

One of the things that has puzzled me for years is the fact that so many of the Christians I meet don't seem especially enthusiastic or excited about life. As a matter of fact, it is virtually impossible much of the time to tell the difference between a Christian and a non-Christian in a busy shopping mall or department store. There's just not much "expectation of the dawn" on our faces. Somehow we flounder through the days so depressed with what might have been—loaded down with yesterday's baggage—and so filled with anxiety about tomorrow that we have no sense of enthusiasm or excitement for the present. We've gotten so busy in the scramble for existing that we have forgotten the wonder of life itself.

### A "Marvelous" Encounter

Few writers have the gift of storytelling to equal Arthur Gordon. In his magnificent book, entitled *A Touch of Wonder,* he tells about getting up one morning depressed and troubled. No big crisis confronted him, but an accumulation of little things had been nibbling at his comfort zone for days on end.

The morning wore on, and things just weren't going well. When the mail came, there was nothing but window envelopes with bills in them. The day was a loser.

Needing urgently to escape the depressive atmosphere of his study, Arthur gathered up a couple of fishing rods and headed toward the seashore, where his boat was tied up: "And on the path leading down to the boat I met my friend the rabbi, walking his dogs. Or rather, my acquaintance the rabbi. We didn't know each other well. In his seventies, recently retired, he had a wonderful face, clean-shaven and strong. Pacing along with his terriers on a tandem leash, he might have been an English squire out for a stroll.

"He glanced at the two long surf rods—I always carry a spare—and then at the skiff riding offshore. 'Fishing? Alone?'

"I nodded, and spoke jokingly: 'Want to come?'

"He looked at me thoughtfully. 'Do you want company?'

"I stared at him, taken back. I was not at all sure that I wanted to share my flight with anyone. And I was quite sure that the rabbi knew as much about surf-fishing as I knew about the Talmud. Still, I *had* asked him."

A few minutes later, Arthur and the rabbi were bouncing along in the skiff on their way to the sandbar about a mile offshore. As they approached the bar, the boat took a big wave at an angle and crashed down into the trough on the other side.

Arthur thought his friend would be terrified, but instead the rabbi's eyes sparkled as he said, "Marvelous! Marvelous!"

They landed on the bar, and when the rabbi saw the "sculptured sand patterns" made by the waves at high tide—"Marvelous . . . The footprints of the sea." And a little later, he found a shell that still had "the sunrise in it."

When they started fishing, Arthur made the first cast for him. The rabbi tried it a couple of times, and then disaster struck as the line became a hopeless tangle from a backlash.

Arthur took the rod to see what might be done and handed the rabbi his own. Moments later a big bass struck, and the reel whined as the line raced out. Through it all the rabbi was hanging on for dear life.

The drama of the next few minutes was a comedy of errors. The rabbi stumbled and fell into the surf, and the rod flew out of his hands. Much to Arthur's amazement, when his friend recovered it, the fish was still there. The tables were turned, though; the bass was playing the fisherman rather than the other way around. Then, at the rabbi's most awkward moment, the great bass reversed its course, the leader snapped, and the fish was gone.

"The rabbi came up beside me. He was soaked, bedraggled, trembling, but there was no defeat in his eyes, no disappointment. 'Marvelous!' he said hoarsely. 'Marvelous.'" And when they parted on the shore, the rabbi thanked Arthur for "one of the great mornings of my life."[3]

## *The Flavor of Enthusiasm*

To the seventy-year-old rabbi on the home stretch, all of life was "marvelous!" He lived "in expectation of the dawn." There is something about enthusiastic people like the rabbi that adds flavor to every stage of life—and especially during the rich home-stretch years. And since this is true, we may find it helpful to move in and take a look at some of those qualities of life that seem to be common to enthusiastic people. What kind of people are they?

(1) *Enthusiastic people usually have a wide variety of interests.* They are not one dimensional but are constantly curious and involved in different activities. Cecil Osborne, in his wonderful book, *The Art of Becoming a Whole Person,* refers to the ninety-eight-year-old retired minister who said that "his happiness in retirement was based on 'being as curious as a stray cat in a strange warehouse.' "[4]

Along with being incurably curious, a person with wide interests has a vivid sense of wonder, an insatiable desire to try new things. This is a carryover from childhood that none of us should have lost. I like to think this is at least part of what Jesus had in mind when, in responding to a question put to him by his disciples as to who is greatest in the kingdom of heaven, he said, "Hear the truth. Unless your hearts are changed and you become as little children, you will not enter the Kingdom of Heaven at all" (Matt. 18:3, Rieu).

What a marvelous comparison! The young child is always trying new things, is constantly exploring with an open mind unclouded by cynicism. Scientist Thomas Huxley understood this truth when he said, "The secret of genius is to carry the spirit of the child into old age." I think we learn from this that we are to be childlike in our interests but not childish in our attitudes. I like Cecil Osborne's observation: "Those who retain an open-eyed sense of wonder and appreciation will never grow old mentally."[5]

(2) *Enthusiastic people have a great capacity for enjoying life.* Over nineteen hundred years ago, the noted Greek biographer Plutarch observed, "For the wise man, every day is a festival." I think that is at least part of the idea behind Jesus' words: "I came so that they will have life and have it overflowing in them" (John 10:10, Beck).

I believe that anyone who has the overflowing life of Christ in them is enthusiastic and really enjoys life! And when we enjoy life, it shows—our enjoyment moves out with a powerful energy that those around us can feel. It is attractive and winsome. And we get a lift by being around other people who enjoy life; we're influenced by them. They make a difference in our lives.

Over and over again in the Gospel stories of Jesus,

we read that people followed after him. He was always surrounded by a crowd. One of the reasons for that, I think, is that he enjoyed life and was interested in all that went on around him.

Then, too, we read in Jesus' story that he was entertained at dinner parties and social events. And he evidently had a good time, even though his fellow guests weren't always those from inside temple and synagogue circles. I'm sure that Jesus' hosts were not much different than we are today—we don't invite duds and bores to our dinners or parties. Instead, we want to associate with people who are interesting, who are *alive* in every way.

I sometimes think that our Christian influence in today's world could be revolutionized for good and for God if so many of us would stop acting as if life is painful, a chore, something to be endured on our way to heaven—and looking as if we had just taken a big bite out of a lemon.

(3) *Enthusiastic people are at ease and comfortable with themselves.* They are not loaded down with the baggage of anxiety and fearfulness. I have to believe that one of the most self-assured and self-confident people in the New Testament is the apostle Paul. He was not fearful nor anxious nor insecure because he knew who he was. He exemplified these words he wrote to his Christian friends at Corinth: "For if a man is in Christ he becomes a new person altogether—the past is finished and gone, everything has become fresh and new" (2 Cor. 5:17, Phillips).

**57**

What a marvelous bit of good news that is! As Christians, we are becoming new persons. When we are in Christ, every day is fresh and new. In him, we have a security that enables us to be at ease and comfortable with ourselves, confident of our status as children of God. But this isn't a security that lulls us into taking it easy or playing it safe. Instead, like the eighty-four-year-old lady in Seattle, we find ourselves becoming bolder, willing to risk for God and trust him because we are secure in his love.

(4) *Enthusiastic people are effective witnesses to a life-changing faith in Jesus Christ.* Earlier I mentioned the crippled beggar at the gate of the temple. Luke wrote that after he was healed, "everyone noticed him . . . and recognised him." He was really turned on, and everybody knew it. They paid attention to him.

Have you ever noticed how easy it is to pass over or ignore a dull and listless person? Some people just fade into the background. If there is anything that turns me off, it is going into a store and being confronted by a halfhearted, negative, and insecure salesperson. I don't think any of us would be particularly impressed if we walked into an automobile salesroom and a salesman eased up and asked in a listless monotone, "You wouldn't want to buy a Buick, would you?" Buy a Buick from him? Never! I won't even go into a 7-Eleven for a jar of pickles unless the sales clerk is enthusiastic about his or her job.

This is why I am attracted by that healed beggar in the story. I wish Luke had told us his name. I'd like to know more about him and what happened after that memorable day.

## *A Present-Day Model*

One of the most enthusiastic and exciting men I've ever known is Dr. Norman Vincent Peale, for many years the senior minister of historic Marble Collegiate Church in New York City. Probably more than any other living person, Dr. Peale epitomizes what it means to be enthusiastic. In one of his sermons a long time ago, he pointed out that our word *enthusiasm* is derived from two Greek words— *en* and *theos*—meaning in God or full of God. Believe me, when we understand and experience what it means to be full of God, we'll be enthusiastic!

In another one of his sermons, Dr. Peale quoted these words from *The Catholic Layman* magazine: "Every man is enthusiastic at times. One man has enthusiasm for thirty minutes—another has it for thirty days. But it is the man who has it for thirty years who makes a success in life."

This is certainly true, and at eighty-eight Dr. Peale is a living model of an enthusiastic and active lifestyle. Even as I write this, he and Mrs. Peale are planning for an extensive trip to Hong Kong and Southeast Asia. Their enthusiasm for God and for life has infected people in our country and across the world for many years.

But the great good news for you and me is that whether we're twenty, forty, or seventy, it is never too late to start living with the kind of attention-getting enthusiasm that got hold of the healed crippled man at the gate of the temple. God wants all of us to live every day "in expectation of the dawn" and "full of joy."

# Having Friends
# and Being A Friend

*A friend is a person with whom we've chosen to be intimate on a deep level. Masks or defenses are not necessary, because a friend accepts us for who we are. We are accepted whether we're grumpy or out of sorts or nice to be with. There's a deep understanding that draws friends together in a healthy dependency on one another.*

I firmly believe that having friends is one of our greatest gifts and being a friend is God's gift through us to someone else. Friendship is a life-changing ingredient at each turn and on every straightaway of life, but it is on the home stretch that we become increasingly aware of the richness it brings—or the loss we feel because of our earlier carelessness and indifference.

## A Life-Changing Friendship

This whole idea comes alive in vivid color when I think of my friend Margie Hamilton. Let me tell you about this remarkable lady.

## Having Friends and Being a Friend

The setting was our first home high up in the Hollywood hills. The time was over thirty-six years ago. Our daughter Linda Lou was playing badminton in our front yard when Margie and her severely handicapped daughter, Nancy, walked by. Without a moment's hesitation, Linda Lou called out a cheery hello and ran down to where Margie and Nancy were standing. After chatting a moment or two, Linda Lou invited them up for cookies and tea.

When I arrived home from shopping, there they all were in the living room. I recovered quickly from my surprise and joined them in a most memorable visit. It was the beginning of a long and rich friendship that was to mean more to me than I could ever have imagined at the time.

When Thanksgiving time rolled around, Roy and I invited Margie and Nancy to our home for dinner. Then by the time Robin, our "angel unaware," was born, we had become very close. God had arranged a friendship that was to help carry me through my days of agony when we realized that our little Robin was so badly handicapped. Margie, who cared for and loved her own sadly deformed Nancy, became my source of comfort during that long, dark night of the soul. It was Margie who prayed with me and loved me when I was so distraught that I couldn't pray for myself.

That life-changing friendship has enriched my life for these thirty-six years. Yes, our Robin and Margie's Nancy are now both with the Lord, but our friendship has remained close all of this time. I feel just as much at home in her postage-stamp-sized trailer house located in a desert trailer park as she does in our much larger home. Material things don't matter; what counts with each of us is God's marvelous gift of friendship for one another.

## *Acquaintances or Friends?*

And yet one of the sad realities of our late twentieth-century culture is that while most people have acquaintances, so few have real friends. The differences are great!

Acquaintances accept us at their convenience for *what* we are. With them, our masks are always in place, our defenses are up to avoid the chance of being rejected. Acquaintances keep us on edge in our desperate struggle for acceptance and social position. By definition, they are persons we know on a casual level either socially or professionally—people we converse with superficially in the supermarket or at the office or in church or at a party. These are folks with whom we're thrown because of circumstances. We can take them or leave them without being affected much one way or another.

But it's different with a friend. A friend is a person with whom we've chosen to be intimate on a deep level. Masks or defenses are not necessary, because a friend accepts us for *who* we are. We are accepted whether we're grumpy or out of sorts or nice to be with. There's a deep understanding that draws friends together in a healthy dependency on one another.

It is this kind of a friend that is described so vividly by the writer of Ecclesiastes:

> A faithful friend is a secure shelter;
> whoever finds one has found a treasure.
> A faithful friend is beyond price;
> his worth is more than money can buy.
>                               Eccles. 6:14–15, NEB

It is having friends like this writer so beautifully describes and being this kind of a friend that adds richness and grace at every stage of life. But I think friendship is especially important in making the home stretch productive and fulfilling. And for the Christian, having friends and being a friend takes on special meaning as our own lives are enriched and our witness for Christ becomes more effective.

## *Jesus and Friends*

Jesus certainly moved the word *friend* from the ordinary to the extraordinary in these words to his disciples: "This is my commandment: love one another, as I have loved you. There is no greater love than this, that a man should lay down his life for his friends. You are my friends, if you do what I command you. I call you servants no longer; . . . I have called you friends" (John 15:12–15, NEB).

Since Jesus sanctified the word *friend* as he did, and since it is friends that give our lives such shape and meaning, it seems to me that we can all benefit by looking closely now at what it means to be a friend and to have friends. What are those qualities that make a friend?

## A Friend Is a Person Who Listens

I suppose if twelve different people were to respond to that question, there would be twelve different starting places. But the first quality I want to mention is: *A friend is a person who listens to us.* Active and loving listening is the greatest compliment that we can pay to anyone.

For most of us today, listening doesn't come easy. We're so busy "broadcasting" during our waking hours that either we don't have time to listen or we've forgotten how. But listening is an art we can all acquire—*if we choose to.*

Dr. Paul Tournier, the gifted and godly Swiss psychiatrist I've quoted so often, stressed the importance of listening when he wrote, "It is impossible to overemphasize the immense need humans have to be really listened to, to be taken seriously, to be understood. *No one can develop*

**67**

*freely in this world and find life without feeling understood by at least one person"* (italics mine). A friend is that one person.

Authors Floyd and Harriett Thatcher, in writing on the importance of listening and how it is done, explain it this way:

> Hearing is passive; listening is active. Listening demands concentration . . . thinking with the other person . . . attempting to become involved not only with words but with the feelings of the other person . . . listening with head tilted toward the speaker and to what is being said as well as to what isn't being said. In fact, listening is hard work; it requires energy and concentration and involvement with the other person. For us, listening is a meeting of the eyes, the windows of the soul; it is the response of caring; it tries hard to understand at all cost.[2]

Only a friend cares enough to listen like that.

## A Friend Is Interested in What the Other Person Says and Feels

My second quality of a friend is this: *A friend is interested in what the other person says and feels.* Most of us are victims of perhaps the most consuming sickness of our times—the belief that only what we think or believe or feel matters. We are in constant danger of being so preoccupied in getting ahead, in doing *our* thing, in satisfying *our* own desires and needs, that we fail to express interest in the feelings and concerns of others. And yet, one of the true gains of friendship is the giving of ourselves to the interests and feelings of the people around us.

It happened many years ago—during World War II, in fact. I was sitting in the front seat of an airplane on my first U.S. Savings Bond tour as a performer. After a time, I realized that a most unattractive-looking lady had slipped into the seat beside me. Then, as I looked again, I saw that it was Eleanor Roosevelt.

In a few moments, we were deep in conversation. She wanted to know where I was going and what I would be doing. And she listened *ever* so carefully to *every* answer. I was amazed—the First Lady seemed interested in *me!* And she seemed to care about what I was thinking and about what was happening to me. Mrs. Roosevelt had the God-given gift of caring about what I said and felt. And where once I had thought she was unattractive, now she looked beautiful!

When we care enough to be interested in another person's concerns, and when we listen carefully to him or her, we make them feel good. Caring and listening builds other people up—it brings out the best in them.

It is this kind of a friend that helps us affirm our

own worth and to believe in ourselves—yes, and to love ourselves. And this is of profound importance, because linked to our capacity to love ourselves is our ability to love other people.

## A Friend Can Say "I Love You"

The third quality I want to include here is: *A friend is someone who can say in words and actions, "I love you."* Somewhere I read this insightful comment by Christopher Morley: "If we discovered that we had five minutes to say all we wanted to say, every telephone booth would be occupied by people calling other people to stammer that they love them."

Too many of us, men and women alike, have what we call in my home state of Texas the "Good Ol' Boy Syndrome" (and women can have it as well as men!). A Good Ol' Boy is a Texan with a heart as big as his state. You can count on him through thick and thin no matter what, but he's tongue-tied when it comes to expressing his feelings. Now, maybe that's enough for some people. Most of us, though, need to hear the words. No affirmation says quite as much between family members or friends as "I love you."

As a rule, it is this kind of a friend, too, who has learned the importance of touching. So often, when all of the words have been said, a hug or an arm around the shoulder or a pat on the arm is the grand convincer that says, "I'm with you."

## Having Friends and Being a Friend

One of the qualities of an "I love you" friend is that he or she always has time for you. I shudder to think of the number of times I may have brushed somebody off because I was in a hurry or was preoccupied with something I thought was more important. Like many people, I don't handle interruptions very well.

But then one day while reading in the Gospels, I discovered that Jesus never treated people as interruptions. It didn't matter whether he was on the road, in a boat by the lake, or in a quiet place praying, when people "interrupted" Jesus, he became present to them.

Writer Henri Nouwen tells this delightful little story about a friend of his: "A few years ago I met an old professor at the University of Notre Dame. Looking back on his long life of teaching, he said with a funny twinkle in his eyes: 'I had always been complaining that my work was constantly interrupted, until I slowly discovered that my interruptions were my work.' "[3]

The old professor had evidently made the same discovery about Jesus that I had—people were never interruptions. Jesus had time for them; and so people were healed, families were reunited, and men and women came to know God. Slowly, all too slowly, I'm beginning to understand that a friend with a need—whatever it is—must never be an interruption.

I don't know Carl Mays, but he tells a beautiful story out of his own childhood in his little book entitled *Mr. Adams: A Parable for Parents and*

*Others.* As a small boy, Carl became friends with Mr. Adams, a seventy-eight-year-old neighbor. It was a friendship that no one, not even his parents, seemed to understand. But as the story of their conversations moves from one incident to another, we begin to see why young Carl was attracted to his aged neighbor: Mr. Adams always listened to him; he was interested in what the boy said and thought. Mr. Adams always had time for Carl; he believed in the boy. Carl was patiently affirmed when he was right and gently corrected when he was wrong.

There was no generation gap between young Carl Mays and old Mr. Adams. Why? Because Mr. Adams had time for his little neighbor. And because of that, Carl carried beautiful memories of his old friend forward into adult life.[4]

Having time as a friend means writing a note or making a phone call to say "Thank you" or "I love you" or "You did a good job" or "I was just thinking about you and wanted you to know." Having time as a Christian friend means making a faithful commitment to pray for someone with a special need. Only God knows the strength Roy and I received from the prayers of friends during our dark hours of bereavement when we lost our children Robin and Debbie and Sandy.

## The Story of Two Special Friends

There are many different stories in the Bible about outstanding friendships. Perhaps the most quoted one is about David and Jonathan. Then, of course, there's the moving story in the Gospels about Jesus' friendship with Lazarus and Mary and Martha. And while it isn't stated directly, we have to believe there were strong bonds of friendship between the twelve disciples of Jesus. There is just no way these men could have lived together as they did, day in and day out for over three years, without being close friends.

But there is one remarkable story of friendship in the New Testament that intrigues me because of the twists and turns it takes. It is the story of a Jew by the name of Joseph from the island of Cyprus and a Jew named Saul from the sophisticated university city of Tarsus in the Roman province of Cilicia.

Joseph was a Levite. And the Levites of the first century were priests involved in the administration of justice. But evidently, Joseph had become a disciple of Jesus. We first meet him early in the Book of Acts and are introduced to him by his surname, Barnabas (Acts 4:36–37).

Saul, on the other hand, was a highly educated Pharisee. Until he met the Lord in a bright light on the road to Damascus, Saul was a sworn enemy of Barnabas and of the other disciples and friends of Jesus.

It was after Saul's conversion that these two men met. We don't know exactly when they met or how, but it was most likely on Saul's first trip to Jerusalem after his conversion. It must have taken a lot of nerve for Saul to return to Jerusalem as a Christian. The last time he had been there, he had gotten warrants from the high priest that were his authority to hunt down and arrest the Christians he'd heard were active in Damascus. And it was in Jerusalem that he had been "breathing out threatenings and slaughter against the disciples of the Lord" (Acts 9:1).

But now the shoe was on the other foot. Saul was a Christian and back in Jerusalem. He wanted to share his experience with the Lord's disciples there, "but they were all afraid of him, and believed not that he was a disciple" (Acts 9:26). Saul was rejected because of his bad reputation, but Barnabas believed his conversion was real. And when Barnabas vouched for Saul, the rest of the disciples accepted him, too.

That had to be the beginning of Paul and Barnabas's friendship. It is possible they were drawn together because of a certain cultural and religious kinship. But whatever the reason was, Barnabas unselfishly stood up for his new friend. This opened the door for spiritual fellowship and for Saul to witness publicly to his new-found faith. And it was while Saul was preaching fearlessly in Jerusalem that he inspired the hatred of the Greek-speaking Jews to the point that they threatened to kill him. To save his life, Paul's Christian brethren had to whisk him out of town to Caesarea then put him on the road north to Tarsus.

Barnabas surfaced again sometime later, when the leaders in the Jerusalem church sent him to Antioch in Syria to find out what was happening among the Gentiles there who had become Christians. He was so impressed with the opportunity for Christian witness in Antioch that he traveled north to Tarsus for help. There he found the man he was looking for—Saul, whom we now know as Paul—and took him back to Antioch where they worked together in the church for a year.

From that point on, the saga of friendship unravels in high adventure. From Antioch, they made a trip back to Jerusalem. Then they returned to Antioch, where the two of them and young John Mark left on their first missionary journey. On shipboard and in traveling across the open country of southern Galatia, Paul and Barnabas worked together and ate together. They stayed together even after John Mark, Barnabas' nephew, deserted them and went home. It seemed their friendship deepened with each passing mile. The two men complemented each other; and Barnabas, sensing Paul's great ability, selflessly deferred to the leadership of his friend.

After returning to Antioch for a time, the two friends laid plans for their second missionary trip together. Barnabas expressed his desire to take John Mark with them again—he wanted to give his nephew a second chance. But Paul would have no part of that. After all, he felt, Mark had been a quitter on their last trip—and once was enough.

So sharp was the disagreement and difference of opinion between Paul and Barnabas that they separated, and we have no record that they ever traveled together again. Barnabas and Mark went off in one direction. Paul, with his new traveling companion, Silas, went in another.

Luke, as he wrote about this sad ending of a friendship, does not comment further about the separation in the Book of Acts. But we have to believe that these two sensitive and godly friends felt their separation deeply. Someone has wisely said that "to lose a friend is to die a little." I have to believe that after going through all they had together, Paul and Barnabas died a little over the breakup of their close and intimate relationship.

I also have to believe that this quarrel ultimately found the kind of healing that only the Lord can bring. It definitely appears that some years after this incident the relationship between Mark and Paul was repaired, for Paul mentions him in his closing words to the Christians in Colossae (Col. 4:10). And if Mark and Paul became friends again, it doesn't take too much imagination to believe that the rift between Paul and Barnabas was healed also.

## A Friend Is Loyal

Friendship is always a risk, and Barnabas risked a great deal when he became the defender and friend of the newly converted Saul of Tarsus. From that time on, until their tragic break, Barnabas loyally boosted his friend's welfare with no apparent thought of his own position. Barnabas was exactly the kind of friend that Paul needed during those early days of his Christian experience. And while we'll not make a judgment as to who was right and who was wrong in their clash, it is not impossible that loyalty to his young nephew Mark was what caused Barnabas to stand firm in his disagreement with Paul. And most certainly, *a friend is a person who is loyal to those he or she loves.* Barnabas may have felt that Mark needed the steady hand of his friendship at that moment far more than Paul did. And it may well be it was because of the influence of his uncle Barnabas that Mark, in the years to come, was able to be a loving comforter to Paul during his last harsh prison days in Rome (2 Tim. 4:11).

### *"Friend" in Chinese*

My friend Dr. Ted Engstrom, who for many years has been president of World Vision, has written a beautiful little book entitled *The Fine Art of Friendship.* In his introduction, he writes,

On a recent trip to Hong Kong, I decided to do something about my gross lack of knowledge about a language now spoken by almost one-fourth of our world's people. I spent an evening with a close friend who is also a scholar of the Chinese language. In two hours, he took me on a breathtaking whirlwind oral tour of China and its more than five thousand years of history. During the course of our visit, we discussed the Chinese word for "friend."

The current, everyday word for *"friend"* in China today is *peng yu,* but its history goes back many centuries. My tutor drew a primitive Chinese character that represented the magnificent tail of a bird called "Phoenix." This bird was so marvelous in detail that the written character came to mean something much more than "Phoenix." It slowly developed into a more generic meaning of "completeness . . . the sum total of physical beauty."

My friend proceeded to tell me that throughout the ensuing years, the literal meaning of the word was completely lost while the written character took on today's meaning of "friend, friendship, or close association."

"Why was that?" I asked.

Outer, visible beauty arrests our attention to be sure, but the true, inner beauties in people—the elegance, truth, and consistency that live within the soul of a friend—are irresistible. In friendships hearts relate to each other.[5]

## *The Building of Memories*

It is in this relating to each other—the lasting impact of deep friendship on our lives—that multiplies its gift over and over again in the form of another of life's great gifts, the gift of memories. Somewhere author John Claypool made this penetrating observation: "A person without a memory is only half a person." If that is true, then it is equally true that a Christian with a memory is a whole person. And all of us strive with God's help and the help of our families and friends to be whole persons.

I've often wished I had been more sensitive earlier in life to building memories—memories that grow out of experiences and relationships. Close friendships may move into the distance because of a change of physical location or even death, but in our memories they remain close and alive and continue to enrich our lives.

## A Gift We Choose to Accept

It is unfortunate, I think, that in the earlier stretches and turns of our lives we are often oblivious to the idea that every day we live is a time for the developing of friends and experiences that can be enriching on our home stretch. We are building memories every day that have the potential for future enrichment and meaning.

Yes, having friends and being a friend is a special kind of a gift, but as with any gift, we have to choose to accept it. And then, after accepting it, we must nurture and cultivate it in order to experience the full joy and meaning that it can bring to the home stretch of our lives.

As I've been writing this chapter, I've thought frequently about the powerful influence friends have had on my own life—how they've shaped and changed it and enriched it. At the same time, I've been painfully aware of lost opportunities for both receiving and giving friendship. Happily, though, I've also seen that my friendship book is never closed. Such being the case, I'm listing for my benefit (and, hopefully, yours) the kind of a person we need to become in order to be a friend whose "worth is more than money can buy."

## To Be a Friend, We Must . . .

• *Develop and maintain an avid interest in other people.* What they think and feel is more important in the relationship than what we will get out of it.

• *Not develop relationships out of selfish motives.* We don't think of our friends as rungs up the ladder of social or professional success.

• *Learn to be active and creative listeners.* This is an art most of us will have to work at to develop. We "hear" sounds and voices, but we "listen" to people—to what they say and how they feel.

• *Have time for other people and not consider them interruptions.* An examination of our day-to-day routines might reveal that most of our time is spent in pursuit of selfish needs and wants. I don't believe this is what the Lord had in mind when he gave us twenty-four hours a day to learn how to live.

• *Be positive and affirm other people.* Ask God to show *us* the good in others and leave everything else up to him. Practice the art of encouragement.

• *Feel free to tell our friends that we love them and appreciate them.* The kind of love Jesus said we should have for our "neighbor" is not a mere sentimental emotion. Rather, it is patient, kind, lasting—not threatened by the success of another nor cooled off by the weaknesses and failures of a friend.


## Friendship Evangelism

As Christians, the Lord has called us to be his witnesses. In response to that call, evangelism has taken many shapes over the centuries. But I wonder now, in this impersonal time in which we live, if perhaps our most effective form of witnessing at every stage, but especially in the home stretch, may be *friendship evangelism.*

# Creative Disciples
# of Change and Growth

*Living a life full of purpose calls for us to be on the move. This is not a rocking-chair-with-a-shawl-over-the-shoulders kind of existence. Rather, it holds before us at all times the adventure of change and growth, the adventure of learning and of doing new things.*

"I like being seventy-five," she exclaimed, "but I will say that aging is not for sissies."[1]

That perceptive comment was part of a conversation between author Elizabeth Yates and her seventy-five-year-old friend, Dr. Margaret Henrichsen. But as I've thought about it, the aging process in all of us began on the day we were born. And I've decided that aging is not for the fainthearted at any stage of life if we grow and change and change and grow the way the Lord intends for us to do.

I remember, as I'm sure you do, the painful process of aging in the adolescent and teenage years. And then we all do a lot of aging during those fun but difficult years when our children are growing up. Some of us felt intense pain and fear on our fortieth birthday—and our fiftieth wasn't much fun either! I don't want to discourage any of you who haven't reached those last two milestones, but aging most certainly is not for timid people! And if this is true in the earlier turns and straightaways of our lives, it is especially true in the home-stretch years.

No, aging is not for sissies if we are to grow and mature and adjust to the inevitable changes that confront us as we strive to live creative and useful lives—*all* of our lives.

## *Coasting or Living with Purpose*

But, unfortunately, so many folks slide into neutral or even reverse when they hit the home stretch. In a charming article about seventy-year-old Dr. Jonas Salk, philosopher, biologist, and developer of the first polio vaccine, writer Joan Wixen quotes the eminent scientist: "At one time, our biggest problems concerned diseases like poliomyelitis. Now we are becoming aware of another type of problem, the acute disorders of minds facing uselessness, highly developed minds suddenly without use or purpose.

"However, this doesn't have to be a problem of old age if people continue to grow as human beings and make life meaningful whether they are employed or not. Unemployment and retirement without constructive purpose are unnatural. . . . Without a constructive purpose life becomes destructive."[2]

## Creative Disciples of Change and Growth

But living a life full of purpose calls for us to be on the move. This is not a rocking-chair-with-a-shawl-over-the-shoulders kind of existence. Rather, it holds before us at all times the adventure of change and growth, the adventure of learning and of doing new things.

I can't begin to tell you the number of times I've heard someone say to a retired friend, "I thought you were going to slow down and take it easy— enjoy life." But slowing down and taking it easy is the best way to grow old in a hurry. As Maggie Kuhn so wisely said, old age is not chronology. Rather it is a state of mind; it's a matter of self-image.

### Taking Change in Stride

Now, I don't believe I've ever known anyone who didn't *want* to have a good self-image and a healthy state of mind. I don't believe anyone deliberately sets out to be negative. I think most of us want to grow old gracefully—to be constructively useful in *every* turn and straightaway of life. But living with grace and adventure and with a constructive purpose is "not for sissies" because it calls for us to become creative disciples of *change* and of *growth*.

Heraclitus, a very wise Greek philosopher who lived about five hundred years before Christ, made an astute observation for which he is famous to this day: No one can step twice into the same river, for it is always changing.

## Creative Disciples of Change and Growth

And what is true of rivers is even more true of life. To resist change is to stagnate, to become uninteresting and dull. To fight change at any stage in life is to stop growing, to become gnarled and stunted. I certainly agree with writer Gail Sheehy, who wrote, "If we don't change, we don't grow. If we don't grow, we are not really living. Growth demands surrender of security. It may mean giving up familiar but limiting patterns, safe and unrewarding work, values no longer believed in, relationships that have lost their meaning."[3] But so often, in Goethe's words, "Everybody wants to be somebody; nobody wants to grow"—because growing is "not for sissies."

### *The Romance of the New*

Somewhere I read this unidentified comment: "If you think you know all about something, you're old. And if you believe you are now doing something as well as it can be done, you are old. But if you are glad to admit that you know but little about anything, you are young."

Being open to change, to learning and doing new things, is what gives the home-stretch years a great spirit of youth and adventure. This is a time for experiencing the romance of the new, for expanding our interests and broadening our horizons. It is a time for striving to do old things better and to do new things well.

## Creative Disciples of Change and Growth

A perfectly marvelous example of that can be seen in a friend of ours in Waco, Texas. Just recently, a newspaper release lauded our friend for shooting his age in eighteen holes of golf—eighty-eight. And this same friend is taking a quick course in conversational Chinese in preparation for a trip to China this year. Best of all, we didn't know he was eighty-eight until we read his golf score. We had him pegged for around seventy.

Admittedly, as we move into midlife and sort of get grooved in to doing certain things in certain ways, we tend to become set in our life patterns. We eat the same food, frequent only certain restaurants, vacation in the familiar and comfortable places where we've been before, visit with the same people, and read the same magazines and only those writers who share our particular points of view.

## Learn New Things

But when we see this happening to us, it is time to set out deliberately to think and do and learn new things—possibly even things we've never done before. The sculptor Michelangelo, at ninety, having lost his eyesight, ran his hand over the statues in St. Peter's Cathedral in Rome and exclaimed, "I can still learn."

In the delightful little book entitled *How to Be Your Own Best Friend,* the authors write to this idea:

**89**

## Creative Disciples of Change and Growth

"If we all just kept on doing exactly what we've done up to now, people would never change, and people are changing all of the time. That's what growth is: doing things you've never done before, sometimes things you once didn't even dream you could."[4]

A friend of ours, a delightful lady in her home-stretch years, had always attended the eleven o'clock service in her church. But one day she was told that the order and form of service was quite different at the nine o'clock hour. She thought this new experience might be interesting and exciting, so she switched; and as far as we know, she still worships at the earlier time. I like her eagerness to have new experiences even though they may involve new routines.

Then there are people we know who, in their late fifties and early sixties, have gone back to school and finished their college education or have taken graduate work. Others, like our Waco friend, have learned a new foreign language or taken a course in creative writing. Some of the most delightful children's books to be published in recent years were written by Mrs. Dorothy Hamilton, a retired Indiana school teacher. Her first book was published after she was sixty. She then went on to write over twenty more to the delight of children throughout the Midwest.

In an Associated Press release of May 1985, the writer quoted Miss Ruth Clark, age ninety-seven:

# Creative Disciples of Change and Growth

We believe in plenty of laughs and many interests, the first of which for me was music. In my opinion, it is the continuing interest in a variety of subjects . . . that greatly enhances one's life, makes living a joy and tends to smooth over the rough spots in life that everyone must learn to endure.

Incidently, Miss Clark's other interests include oceanography and the Boston Red Sox baseball team.[5]

Then I read about another lady who is sixty-nine years old and "has more unfinished projects stacked in various places in her cluttered workroom than she can keep up with." Her interest in learning has evidently been lifelong and includes extensive research and writing on the Indians of Texas.

And in our own case, it would be very easy to settle down in the ease and comfort of our Apple Valley home. But Roy keeps quite busy at the Roy Rogers Museum in Victorville, and he travels some for the Marriott Corporation, which holds the franchises to the Roy Rogers Family Restaurants. He is also connected with Thousand Trails, a campground for travelers. And as I write this we are about to break ground for the first Roy Rogers-Dale Evans Happy Trails Resort near Phoenix. In addition to all of this, I travel a great deal, speaking and appearing on television. Life is an adventure for us, even though we're both on the other side of that three score and ten. And we'll keep it up as long as the good Lord gives us health and strength.

## *The Ability to Dream and Use Imagination*

Another part of the growth process that can enrich our lives and in turn enable us to enrich the lives of others is our ability to dream and freely use our imagination during our midlife and home-stretch years. So often along about that time, we have a tendency to look back, live in the past, and yearn for what we label the "good old days."

It is true as we said earlier that memories are important, but only as they help us live more vibrantly in the present and in the future. To live in the past is a horrible waste of God's creative energy. And besides, I'm not so sure the good old days were all that good. I remember my childhood days in Italy, Texas, without air conditioning and 110 degrees in the shade—when you could find it. Those days weren't all so good! Frankly, I think *now* is the great time to be alive.

It is thrilling to live in the time of space exploration. I still get goose bumps when we see pictures on our television screens of Saturn and Uranus taken by spacecraft and relayed millions of miles back to earth. And to see close-up pictures of Halley's Comet taken from a spaceship is a once-in-a-lifetime experience, since the comet makes its appearance only every seventy-six years or so.

## Creative Disciples of Change and Growth

Yes, now is a very special time to be alive, especially as we view the present and look forward to the years ahead. Today, as never before, though, our true age lies in the lifespan ahead, not in the past.

I remember so well the lyrics to a song that was popular many years ago: "When I grow too old to dream . . ." Nonsense! I don't believe God wants us to grow too old to dream, to use our imaginations, to look expectantly into the future. The whole and very alive person plans eagerly for the future. He or she doesn't travel bumper to bumper but keeps looking far ahead down life's road with an eye toward what is just beyond the next hill or around the next turn.

I was delighted this year when my husband, Roy, planted some young fruit trees in the "back forty" of our deep lot bordering on the golf course in Apple Valley. It will probably be several years before those trees even begin to bear fruit. But Roy is always planning for the future.

## *Growth through Struggle*

It is true, of course, that our view of the future doesn't always come from a vantage point of ease. We are frequently plagued with hard and difficult times, but it is out of these that we grow and mature and are able to view the future with expectancy. One particular author expressed this idea well although he wasn't writing from a Christian perspective: "It is only through struggling with the pain of our own crises, tragedies, sins, depressions, and problems that our greatness as human beings is realized. Our crises are anvils on which our growth is forged."[6]

But as our growth is forged on the anvil of experience, we can discover our capacity to dream and to use our imaginations creatively to the enrichment of our own lives and to the delight of others. Our imaginations deal with the *might-be* element in our lives.

So many of us, though, have allowed the so-called realities of life to so sterilize our minds and emotions that we've forgotten how to dream dreams and see visions—to draw on the richness of the world of make-believe. Referring back to the story of the little eagle who was raised as a chicken—our minds and God-given imaginations are meant to soar like an eagle, not to be used to peck around for corn in the dirt and muss of the chicken yard.

### Enriching Imagination

One of the most delightful stories that pictures the richness that can be ours if we exercise our imaginations during our home-stretch years is told by Dr. Wayne Oates. Dr. Oates is a prominent counselor, psychologist, and professor in a graduate school of medicine. But he possesses the marvelous gift of a vivid and creative mind and imagination, even though he, too, is in the home stretch.

He writes,

> I was playing with our four-year-old grandson, Will, the other day. He loves to use our king-size bed as a trampoline. This time his feet were dirty, and I asked him to let me first wash his feet. Then he could jump on the bed.
>
> I took a warm and wet washcloth and washed his feet. Then I took the cloth to the bathroom to wash the dirt out of it. When I returned, Will was gone. I assumed he had gone out of the bedroom. Hence, I went about hanging a suit up and placing some shoes in the closet.
>
> Suddenly he jumped from behind the bed where he had been hiding. I reacted with great surprise, saying: "Where on earth did you come from, and how did you get in this room?" He said: "I came through that wall right there!" I said: "Well, I don't see any hole in the wall." He said: "I know. I fixed it back just like it was and painted it this color," pointing to a special color in the wallpaper. "And," he said, "if you will touch it with your finger, you will see that it's still wet paint." I reached and touched it with my finger and looked at my finger and said: "My goodness! You're right! It *is* still wet!" At which point both of us broke into hilarious laughter together. What fun! What magic![7]

Yes, that is a warm little story about a man and his grandson. But the point is that neither the grandfather nor his grandson will ever lose the warmth and richness of those magic moments, and both will be better people for having lived them. For both, the process of growth is wonderfully enhanced by their ability to think imaginatively and to dream.

## *The Drama of Optimism*

There's another attractive quality of life that seems peculiar to "people on the grow"—they are alive with optimistic energy. In fact, I believe that growth and an openness to change can only be experienced by a person who is an optimist at heart.

To see the bright side of life, to look to the future with confidence and hope, is not to deny the difficult and rough times. Rather, it is to expect the best possible outcome or to dwell on the most hopeful aspects of any situation. And for the Christian, this definition is intimately a reality in Jesus Christ.

The drama of changing and growing as a person is nurtured by optimism and hope. Author Henri Nouwen has said, "An important part of the spiritual life is to keep longing, waiting, hoping, expecting."[8] This kind of a spirit is not for sissies as we wrestle with the growing process in the midlife and home-stretch years. Life is an ongoing journey of becoming.

It is the joyful and optimistic Christian who is alive to the opportunities for personal growth and is able to cope with the strains of life. And it is the Christian who has learned to dream and be imaginative and have an expectant and hopeful view of the future who, with God's help, can handle Evelyn Underhill's definition of what it means to be spiritually mature and alive:

> To be spiritually alive means to be growing and changing; not to settle down among a series of systemized beliefs and duties, but to endure and go on enduring the strains, conflicts and difficulties incident to development.
>
> Even the greatest spiritual teachers such as St. Paul and St. Augustine could never afford to relax the tension of their own spiritual lives; they never seem to stand still, are never afraid of conflict and change.[9]

## The Christian on the Move

Picking up on what Evelyn Underhill has said, I would add that the growing Christian does not stand still; there is no relaxing. God doesn't intend for us to settle down and take it easy in any one place. This idea is wonderfully illustrated many places in the Bible, but two stories particularly stand out in my mind.

First, there's the story of Peter, James, and John, who had the awesome experience of being with Jesus on the mountaintop when he was transfigured. While Jesus was praying, "the aspect of his face was changed and his clothing became brilliant as

**97**

lightning" (Luke 9:29, JB). Next, the three disciples saw Moses and Elijah with Jesus and overheard their conversation. This was a once-in-a-lifetime experience, and Peter immediately wanted to memorialize the event by building three monuments to mark the spot. But that was not to be; in a few moments, the scene had changed and Jesus was alone.

It wasn't lasting memorials that God wanted, but healed and changed lives. We shouldn't be too critical of Peter, though, because so often we face a similar temptation. We want to memorialize our spiritual high points and then go back to them again and again. But instead, as the disciples of Jesus learned, we are to be on the move—to grow and press ahead for new experiences.

Then there is the wonderful Old Testament story of the Tabernacle—God's first "dwelling place" within Israel. After the Hebrews had gotten settled in Canaan, there were those who felt that the portable tabernacle should be replaced by a permanent building—a temple like those stately buildings that their neighbors had constructed to the pagan gods. But it was too soon for such a structure. Israel's God was active and on the move. He was not to be restricted to one spot. In his plan, this was not a time for memorials.

It wasn't until much later that God allowed a temple to be built that would serve as his "dwelling place" among the people. But even that majestic temple did not last forever; it was leveled first by the armies of Babylon and then by those of Rome. The God of Israel and our God can never be confined to buildings, for he is a God of movement, of change, of growth.

## An Example of Growth and Maturity

While the facts are sketchy, the story of John Mark in the New Testament seems to be a wonderful illustration of the transformation that can take place as a person grows in the Christian faith.

We first meet John Mark in the Garden of Gethsemane at the time of Jesus' arrest. It is likely he was about fifteen or sixteen at the time. We don't know how or why Mark was there or why he was apparently wearing nothing more than a sheet wrapped around him. But we do know that there was some kind of a scuffle, and a temple guard evidently tried to hold him. But Mark slipped out of the sheet and escaped naked from the garden.

Mark next appears some fifteen years later as he starts out with his uncle Barnabas and Paul on their first missionary journey. Evidently, he gave a good account of himself as they traveled through Cyprus. But when Paul and Barnabas and Mark landed on the south coast of Asia Minor and the decision was made to proceed north to Antioch of Pisidia, a Roman stronghold, Mark decided to desert his companions. We don't know the reason for his defection, but it is possible that his lack of maturity prompted him to leave rather than undergo the rigors of overland travel (or possibly he feared Roman persecution).

Paul and Barnabas went on alone, and while there was no rift in their relationship at that time, a break came later when Barnabas wanted to take Mark along on their second trip. Paul made it clear then that there was no place in his party for a quitter. His feelings were so strong that Paul and Barnabas separated and went different ways.

After that rather sad scene, Mark's life and activities are clothed in silence, and we have no idea what happened to him during those years. But we can conclude from two later references that he grew and matured as a man and in his Christian faith. After being rejected as a quitter by Paul at the beginning of the second missionary journey, he is next praised by the great apostle as being "profitable to me for the ministry" (2 Tim. 4:11). He is again mentioned by Paul in his letter to Philemon. And, of course, Mark's pilgrimage from immaturity to maturity is wonderfully apparent in the Gospel he wrote that bears his name.

### The Prime Reason for Growth

We have stressed the importance of change and growth for the enrichment of our lives throughout every turn and straightaway and especially in the home stretch. But as Christians, our eyes are always on the future. Somehow I have to believe that our life here is a preparation for the future. In his incomparable style, C. S. Lewis gives us something serious to think about:

> Christianity asserts that every individual human being is going to live forever. . . . Now there are a good many things which would not be worth bothering about if I were going to live only seventy years, but which I had better bother about very seriously if I am going to live forever.[10]

Among those things worth bothering about, I believe, is an openness to change and a determination to grow in every way as we race down every yard of the home stretch.

## Steps to a Rich and Rewarding Life

One of my dreams for many years has been to write a book on the home-stretch years of life. And for me, this is one of the most important chapters in the book. As I've worked through my thinking and feelings, especially in this chapter, certain very important ideas or steps to a rewarding life stand out in my mind. And as my own growth process continues with each new day, I think it will be helpful to be reminded of these high points that can and will move us on toward maturity as persons. I'm convinced that "to think on these things" can add years and zest to our lives:

## Creative Disciples of Change and Growth

• *We are to avoid a "rocking chair" attitude as we move into the midlife and home-stretch years.* Joy in living and life-enriching experiences come from "living on the move."

• *If we don't change, we don't grow—and if we don't grow, we stagnate.* An eager openness to change keeps life exciting.

• *Doing new and unfamiliar things not only adds adventure to our lives, but also makes us interesting people to be with.*

• *We are never to be "too old to dream."* Dreaming dreams, seeing visions, using our God-given imaginations are keys that unlock our doors to the future.

• *To grow is to tackle each new day with optimism.* No one is ever made better by a pessimistic view of life. For the Christian, pessimism is a lack of faith; optimism sees God at work today and tomorrow.

• *The adventure of the future is always with us* as we plan and look ahead expectantly. The past is important only as it prepares us for the future.

The growing person doesn't live in a house with mirrors for walls, but in one with huge windows on every outside wall! It is not when we concentrate on reflections of ourselves, but when we look out into God's wonderful world and into the future, that satisfaction and fulfillment flood our lives and make us effective witnesses for the Lord.

# Quality of Life
# for the
# Home Stretch

*Our concern is for the quality of life rather than the quantity. And for those of us pragmatic and achievement-oriented citizens of this late twentieth-century Western world, this is sorely needed advice. Often we "run our race" with our eyes so glued to the track immediately in front of our feet that all we see is our own particular yard of dirt. We concentrate so heavily on ourselves—our successes, our needs and wants, our satisfaction—that we lose sight of everything else, including the richness of life and relationships that God wants us to have.*

An unknown friar, probably writing in the home stretch of his life, is credited with this profound bit of reflection:

If I had my life to live over, I'd try to make more mistakes next time. I would relax, I would limber up; I would be sillier than I have been on this trip. I know of very few things I would take seriously. I would be less hygienic. I would take more chances. I would take more trips. I would climb more mountains, swim more rivers and watch more sunsets. I would eat more ice cream. I would have more actual troubles and fewer imaginary ones.

You see, I am one of those people who lives prophylactically and sensibly and sanely, hour after hour, day after day. Oh, I have had my moments and, if I had it to do over again, I'd have more of them. In fact, I'd try to have nothing else. Just moments, one after another, instead of living so many years ahead each day.

I've been one of those people who never go anywhere without a thermometer, a hot water bottle, a gargle, a raincoat, and a parachute. If I had it to do over again, I would go places and do things and travel lighter than I have.

If I had my life to live over again, I would start barefooted earlier in the spring and stay that way later in the fall. I would play hooky more; I wouldn't make such good grades except by accident. I would ride on more merry-go-rounds. I would pick more daisies!

I'm just very sure that wise and reflective friar had no intention for this to be taken as a literal autobiographical statement. Instead, I feel quite certain he was writing in parable form in order to express an enormously important truth.

## Quality versus Quantity

He is wanting us, I believe, to be more concerned with the quality of life rather than the quantity. And for those of us pragmatic and achievement-oriented citizens of this late twentieth-century Western world, this is sorely needed advice. Often we "run our race" with our eyes so glued to the track immediately in front of our feet so that all we see is our own particular yard of dirt. We concentrate so heavily on ourselves—our successes, our needs and wants, and our satisfaction—that we lose sight of everything else, including the richness of life and relationships that God wants us to have.

With a somewhat different kind of expression, another unknown writer caught the sense of what I think the friar was trying to say with these words:

> For yesterday is but a dream,
> And tomorrow is only a vision;
> But today well lived makes every
>     yesterday a dream of happiness,
> And every tomorrow
>     a vision of hope.

Today well lived—this is what counts. It is the quality of life at each straightaway and turn that determines the quality at each future stage.

## A Modern Example

One of the great present-day examples of the quality of life and a vision of hope is Claude Pepper, for many years a United States senator from Florida and now a member of the House of Representatives. At eighty-five, Claude Pepper is a dynamo in the United States Congress; he possesses a unique sense of humor. In an Associated Press release, the reporter wrote, "Despite two hearing aids, triple-focus glasses, a pacemaker in his chest, and two plastic valves in his heart, Pepper says he enjoys the daily challenges he encounters as chairman of the House Rules Committee and subcommittee chairman of the House Select Committee on Aging."

And then the reporter quoted Mr. Pepper directly: "I can't run ten miles in the afternoon, like I did in college, but I have a good car to take me there."[1]

Mr. Pepper's todays are "well lived" and his every tomorrow is obviously "a vision of hope." He has been heard to comment that he would be dead today if he had been forced to retire at sixty-five. He was not a victim of the idea that a person is a leftover at the age of sixty-five. Instead of slowing down as he moved into the home stretch, his pace picked up and the quality of his life became even richer as he pursued causes that he believes in with a passionate zeal. People like Mr. Pepper are *needed* and will be long remembered and revered for their energetic contribution to the welfare of others.

### A Tragic Contrast

In vivid contrast to the relaxed and reflective friar and the dynamic Claude Pepper is the tragic story of an intense Old Testament king of Judah by the name of Jehoram. Unlike his father, King Jehoshaphat—who did "that which was right in the sight of the Lord" (2 Chron. 20:32)—Jehoram was a real rascal. When he became king on the death of his father, he was thirty-two years old and obviously very insecure—in addition to having a perverted sense of what was right and wrong. One of his first acts after being crowned king was to kill off all possible opposition, including members of his own family.

Jehoram's eight-year reign was a succession of one evil act after another—it was a black time in Judah's history. But at the age of forty, he died an agonizing death from a loathsome and incurable disease that had plagued him for two years. The writer of 2 Chronicles 21:19–20 says, "His people made no burning for him"—(there was no time of mourning) and he "departed without being desired" (he was no longer wanted or needed; they were glad to see him die). The quality of Jehoram's life was such that he left nothing good behind him and nobody missed him or was sorry that he was gone. This has to be the ultimate tragedy!

One of our deepest longings in life is to feel needed and wanted—to feel that someone cares, that we have worth to them. But in contrast to Jehoram's self-centered and evil lifestyle, feelings of worth come from having a full and rich life—the kind Jesus promised (John 10:10) and wants us to enjoy. And all of this becomes possible, I believe, by practicing a lifestyle symbolized in the reflections of the friar quoted at the beginning of this chapter.

## *A Healthy Perspective*

A quality of life that can make a positive difference is epitomized not by the traveler who always takes "a thermometer, a hot water bottle, a gargle, a raincoat, and a parachute" when he travels, but by one who wants to "ride on more merry-go-rounds." This is a person with a healthy perspective, a sense of humor—one who doesn't take himself too seriously. It is as "we pick more daisies" that we are open to the fullness of God and the exuberant joy he wants us to have.

Now, don't misunderstand me. We *are* to take God seriously. But this doesn't mean living as if the weight of the world was on *our* shoulders, as if God's mission in the world depended *only* on us and our sobriety. So often, instead of clustering joyfully with people in search of God, we draw apart with pained expressions on our faces and talk with a somber tone and inflection in language that is foreign to any except those who are a part of our particular "in group."

In his book entitled *The Humor of Christ,* Dr. Elton Trueblood quotes from an old pamphlet, entitled *God in Everything,* published by Epworth Press. Parson John is writing to Miriam Gray and says,

> Many of the religious people that I know, when they talk of religion, have a bedside manner and walk

about in felt slippers. And if they speak of God they always tidy themselves first. But *you* go in and out of all the rooms in God's house as though you were quite at home. You open the doors without knocking and you hum on the stairs, and it isn't always hymns either. My aunt thinks you are not quite reverent; but then, she can keep felt slippers on her mind without any trouble.

Dr. Trueblood then goes on to stress the fact that the Christian is to be full of joy, even in the midst of difficult circumstances, because he or she knows that God's purposes will ultimately be accomplished.[2]

It seems to me that a quality of life that enriches our midlife and home-stretch years and in turn helps us to make life better for others is a healthy sense of humor that helps us to keep ourselves in a proper perspective. It is fun to be around a person who enjoys life and can see its humorous side as well as its serious one. In fact, I believe it is this kind of person who witnesses most effectively to the goodness and greatness of God. People don't find Christ in buildings, but in other people—attractive and winsome people who enjoy themselves and others.

I like the kind of humor and sense of purpose expressed by a Catholic sister I read about somewhere: "We can't sit here forever and listen to our arteries harden. We have to get out of our little nunny world." Or, picking up on Parson John's comments as quoted by Elton Trueblood—we've got to get the felt slippers off of our minds and be about the joy of living in a big world. As Bishop Fulton Sheen once said, "The amount of humor that anyone gets out of the world is the size of the world in which he lives." And God has set us down in a *big* world.

## Accentuate the Positives

Throughout all of life, but especially at midlife and then on into the home stretch, our lives are meant to be full of good humor, of the fullness of joy— we are to "make a joyful noise unto the Lord" (Ps. 98:4). But so often the quality of our lives suffers because we concentrate on the negatives. Joy Davidman opens her readable and provocative book, *Smoke on the Mountain,* with this thought-provoking story:

There is a tale told of a missionary in a dark corner of Africa where the men had a habit of filing their teeth to sharp points. He was hard at work trying to convert a native chief. Now, the chief was very old, and the missionary was very Old Testament— his version of Christianity leaned heavily on thou-shalt-not's. The savage listened patiently.

"I do not understand," he said at last. "You tell me that I must not take my neighbor's wife."

"That's right," said the missionary.

**112**

"Or his ivory, or his oxen."

"Quite right."

"And I must not dance the war dance and then ambush him on the trail and kill him."

"Absolutely right!"

"But I cannot do any of these things!" said the savage regretfully. "I am too old. To be old and to be Christian, they are the same thing!"[3]

Our danger as Christians in the home stretch is that so often we act "old." We lose sight, as this missionary evidently had, of the truth that the God of the Old Testament is also the God of the New—that he was and is a God of love as well as justice. As a matter of fact, the "first and great commandment" of Jesus in Matthew 22 is a quotation from both Deuteronomy and Leviticus in the Old Testament.

Contrast the message the African chief got from the missionary and his understanding of it with the attitude of writer Booth Tarkington. When he was seventy-five years old, someone asked whether old people felt old in spirit. "I don't know," he answered. "Why don't you ask someone who is old?" Or with the controversial contemporary scientist Dr. Linus Pauling. We saw him interviewed on television while this chapter was being written. At eighty-five, he was full of life and optimism and held a confident view of the future. In fact, the reason for his appearance was to promote his new book entitled *How to Live Longer and Feel Better.*

# Quality of Life for the Home Stretch

## A Shared Faith

It is this quality of living that gives flavor and color and zest to life, that helps us feel wanted and needed, that gives us the resources to make a difference in the lives of others. Remember, for the Christian, eternal life in Christ is *now,* and it is meant to be rich and fulfilling.

One of the greatest joys of being a Christian comes as we share our faith with our families and those with whom we work and play and worship. But sharing our faith is more than a joy; it is what the Lord instructed us to do. I repeat: people don't meet and discover Christ in buildings but in other people, not in plays and concerts but in performers and actors. Christ isn't discovered merely in people with a Christian label but in "doers of the Word."

But our assignment as Christian witnesses isn't to carry sandwich boards emblazoned with warnings or proof texts. Rather, it is to act and live our faith in the joy of the Lord who makes a difference in each of our worlds.

## A Present Pattern for an Exciting Future

"The straight part of a race track from the last turn to the finish"—the home stretch—calls for our greatest and most creative efforts. It will be IF . . .

## Quality of Life for the Home Stretch

• *We strain ahead for what is still to come and see in each day an adventure of faith.* We have made the deliberate decision to choose life.

• *We don't approach life with a "sneeze mentality"—acting as if life were a series of reflex actions over which we have no control.* It is our attitudes that determine life's meaning and direction. And as Christians, we are to live energized by positive attitudes—we are not grasshoppers in a world of giants, but eagles designed by God to soar.

• *We live with exuberant enthusiasm.* Sam Goldwin, pioneer moviemaker, once said, "Enthusiasm for what you are doing is, I think, the key to success. I know that in picture-making you have to have enthusiasm, love, and affection and excitement about the picture you are making. . . . I have found enthusiasm for work and life to be the most precious ingredient in any recipe for successful living."[4]

This same kind of enthusiasm and optimism shines through in a comment sixty-two-year-old actor Charlton Heston made in a recent interview, "You know, I've been a very lucky man. I have no regrets. There are still lots of roles I want to play, much I want to do. And, inside, I still feel like a young man full of optimism and wonder."[5]

• *We give top priority in our lives to making friends and being a friend.* The writer of Ecclesiastes understood the importance of friendship when he wrote, "Two are better than one, because they have a good reward for their labor. For if they fall, one will lift up his companion. But woe to him who is alone when he falls, for he has no one to help him up. . . . how can one be warm alone?" (4:9–11, NKJV).

Having a friend, being a friend—sometimes a mentor—means we're not alone. It is through friendship that our lives are enriched and our influence on others becomes effective.

• *We remember that growing and maturing in life and in the Christian faith comes from an awareness of being fully alive, an openness to change, and a willingness to dream.* A child asks, "Where did I come from?" A teenager asks, "What shall I do?" The mature person asks, "What shall I become?"

It is a little like looking into a kaleidoscope—when we hold it up to our eye, the beautiful pattern almost takes our breath away. But unless we turn it, we'll miss the beautiful design that comes with the change. This is what life is meant to be like for the growing Christian. As we change and mature, life becomes increasingly beautiful with each change.

To cling to the past, to hang on to the present is to miss the joy of the home stretch. With St. Paul, we forget the past and press on with the words of Jesus always before us, "For whosoever will save his life shall lose it; but whosoever shall lose his life for my sake and the gospel's, the same shall save it" (Mark 8:35).

# Notes

### Chapter 1

1. Viktor E. Frankl, *Man's Search for Meaning* (Boston: Beacon, 1959, 1962), 72.

2. Paul Tournier, *Learn to Grow Old* (Harper & Row, 1972), 12.

3. I have been unable to locate the source for this wonderful story. This omission will gladly be rectified in future printings when and if the source is located.

### Chapter 2

1. Ben Campbell Johnson, *The Heart of Paul: 2 Corinthians 11:23–27* (Waco, TX: Word, 1976), 102.

### Chapter 3

1. C. S. Lewis, *Mere Christianity* (New York: Macmillan/Collier, 1943, 1945, 1952), 117.

2. Bruce Larson, *My Creator, My Friend* (Waco, TX: Word, 1986), 191–192.

3. Arthur Gordon, *A Touch of Wonder* (Old Tappan, NJ: Revell, 1974), 143–148.

4. Cecil G. Osborne, *The Art of Becoming a Whole Person* (Waco, TX: Word, 1978), 85.

5. Ibid., 86.

### Chapter 4

1. Paul Tournier, *To Understand Each Other* (Atlanta: John Knox, 1967), 8.

2. Floyd and Harriett Thatcher, *Long Term Marriage* (Waco, TX: Word, 1980), 83.

3. Henri Nouwen, *Out of Solitude* (Notre Dame, IN: Ave Maria, 1974).

4. The story appeared in *Creative Help for Daily Living* under the title, "The Gift of Friendship," © 1980, Foundation for Christian Living, Pawling, NY.

5. Ted W. Engstrom with Robert C. Larson, *The Fine Art of Friendship* (Nashville: Thomas Nelson, 1985), 13.

### Chapter 5

1. Elizabeth Yates, *Call It Zest* (Brattleboro, VT: Stephen Greene, 1977), 22.

2. Joan Saunders Wixen, "Twentieth Century Miracle Maker," *Modern Maturity,* December 1984–January 1985, 96.

3. Gail Sheehy, *Passages* (New York: Dutton, 1976), 353.

4. Mildred Newman and Bernard Berkowitz with Jean Owen, *How to Be Your Own Best Friend* (New York: Random House, 1971), 19.

5. "Women Reveal Secrets of Longevity," Associated Press article in *Waco Tribune-Herald,* 27 May 1985.

6. Harold C. Lyons, Jr., *Tenderness Is Strength* (New York: Harper & Row, 1977), 23.

7. Wayne E. Oates, *The Struggle to Be Free* (Philadelphia: Westminster, 1983), 162–163.

8. Henri Nouwen, *The Genesee Diary* (New York: Doubleday, 1976).

9. Evelyn Underhill, *The House of the Soul and Concerning the Inner Life* (Minneapolis: Winston-Seabury, 1926, 1929).

10. C. S. Lewis, *Mere Christianity* (New York: Macmillan/Collier, 1943, 1945, 1952), 73.

## *Chapter 6*

1. "85-Year-Old Denounces Retirement," Associated Press article in *Waco Tribune-Herald,* 13 March 1986.

2. Elton Trueblood, *The Humor of Christ* (New York: Harper & Row, 1964), 31–32.

3. Joy Davidman, *Smoke on the Mountain* (Philadelphia: Westminster, 1953, 1954), 13.

4. Sam Goldwin, "Creating with Enthusiasm," *Nation's Business,* November 1966.

5. Dotson Rader, "If I Ran and Won, I'd Never Be Able to Act Again," *Parade,* 9 March 1986.

# Praise for *The Renegade Pastor*

Nelson Searcy is the ultimate renegade pastor. That means that he has a great passion to lead at his highest level—to be different when that's called for, and he *never* settles for average. He is the perfect person to lead you out of the rut of mediocrity so that you can lead to your highest level. *Read this book and abandon average!*

**Jimmy Britt**
Lead Pastor, Rocky River Church, Concord, North Carolina

Wanting to be more than just average or mediocre? Then embed into your life the Seven Commitments of a Renagade Pastor that Nelson shares in this book. It could change your life.

**Bill Easum**
President and Senior Consultant with 21st Century Strategies

Nelson Searcy more than wrote the book on how to do church. He has taken the principles of "how-to-do" from Scripture and made it amazingly doable for the pastor who wants church to be better. Searcy is amazing. He leads. He trains. He equips. He writes. And when he does, some of the most profound principles of leading the greatest enterprise on earth come within reach of you the pastor.

**Dick Hardy**
Founder and President, The Hardy Group www.thehardygroup.org
Author of *Right Turns* and *27 Tough Questions Pastors Ask*

Nelson Searcy loves ministers. I can say this because I've worked with him now for over two decades. This book is an expression of Nelson's heart and passion to help every minister experience a spiritually healthy lifestyle. In my work with thousands of ministers in churches large and small, I can say with assurance that each one would benefit from this book.

**Milton A. Hollifield, Jr.**
Executive Director, Baptist State Convention of North Carolina

*The Renegade Pastor* shows church leaders how to move their life and ministry from average to awesome! Most of us start out with a dream of doing great things for God. The challenges we face often cause this dream to leak out. In this book Nelson Searcy will inspire church leaders to dream again and to dream bigger than ever. It provides valuable advice and tools for overcoming mediocrity and truly become a renegade pastor.

**Steve Reynolds**
Lead pastor, Capital Baptist Church, Annandale, Virginia
Author of *Bod4God* and *Get Off the Couch*

Seminary is an important part of a pastor's preparation for ministry, but there are key areas of pastoral life that seminary doesn't address. *The Renegade Pastor* picks up the loose ends by delving into critical life management issues that every pastor faces. Over the years, I have come to consider Nelson Searcy a friend. I know the man and his work, and I trust both the heart and foundational principles that anchor everything he writes. This book is no exception. If you want to take a step forward in terms of the excellence you bring to your life and ministry, I encourage you to spend some time learning what it means to become a renegade pastor.

**Dr. Elmer Towns**
Co-founder and Vice President, Liberty University
Dean, Liberty Baptist Theological Seminary

I always enjoy reading anything Nelson Searcy writes. He inspires growth in the local church and in church leaders as well. *The Renegade Pastor*, will help you discover ideas that will sharpen you as a leader and help you fulfill the call of God in your life. Nelson defines *The Renegade Pastor* as one who is "passionately abandoned to the plans of God and experiences fulfillment in life and ministry." Every pastor needs a deeper, more personal understanding of both of these areas.

**Philip Wagner**
Pastor, Oasis Church, Los Angeles
PhilipWagner.com

There is an epidemic of defection and defeat among pastors. *The Renegade Pastor* is a book that can help turn the tide. This book is chock-full of practical wisdom that will help pastors "live well" and "lead well." Nelson doesn't write from theory but from years of experience as a local church pastor. What I love about this book is that Nelson doesn't just focus on the "what," he masterfully shows me "how." This book is a must-read for pastors.

**Lance Witt**
Pastor and founder, Replenish Ministries, replenish.net

If you want to be average don't read or apply the principles found in this book. On the other hand if you want to move past stuck and experience momentum in your personal life, relationships and ministry this book is for you! The principles found here have changed my life and the lives of countless others.

**Andy Wood**
Lead Pastor, South Bay Church, Silicon Valley, California

# THE
# Renegade
## PASTOR

ABANDONING AVERAGE IN YOUR LIFE AND MINISTRY

# Nelson Searcy

with Jennifer Dykes Henson

**BakerBooks**

a division of Baker Publishing Group
Grand Rapids, Michigan

Published by Baker Books
a division of Baker Publishing Group
P.O. Box 6287, Grand Rapids, MI 49516-6287
www.bakerbooks.com

Baker Books edition published 2014
Paperback edition published 2015
ISBN 978-0-8010-0049-2

Previously published by Regal Books

Printed in the United States of America

Library of Congress Control Number: 2015930235

15  16  17  18  19  20  21      7  6  5  4  3  2  1

To the members of the Renegade Pastors Network and my coaching network alumni, who model the principles in this book.

# Contents

# Acknowledgments

From Nelson Searcy:

Written as one pastor talking to another pastor, this is my most personal book to date. Can we talk? I hope so! Whether you agree with me, argue with me, or join me on the renegade journey I present in these pages, I am grateful for your ministry, calling and passion to serve God and His local church. Thank you for reading this book.

My eternal gratitude goes to Jesus Christ for calling me to salvation and later to full-time vocational ministry. I'm honored to be one of His equippers for His church. Many years ago, when I first started blogging for pastors, I titled my blog *The Renegade Pastor* because that's how I felt. Little did I know that God would use the phrase as a guidepost for so many of my fellow pastors. To Him be the glory.

I would like to express my sincere appreciation to the team that makes Church Leader Insights, my coaching networks and The Renegade Pastors Network happen every day of every week. You have no idea of the impact you are having on pastors around the world. Thank you, Scott Whitaker, Tommy Duke, Jimmy Britt, Brendan Vinson, Kimberly Pankey, Patricia Garcia, Vinny Bove and David Peterson, plus all of the coaching alumni who serve the Kingdom through our ministry.

It's not an exaggeration to say that this book wouldn't exist without Scott Whitaker. After hearing me say for years that I wanted to build a network of renegade pastors, he finally cornered me (literally) in a hotel lobby in Southern California and told me it was time to put action behind my words (at least that's what I heard him say; I'm

sure he was more tactful). Two months later, The Renegade Pastors Network was born—and now this book. Thank you, Scott!

A huge thanks also to my colleagues at The Journey Church, both past and present. Since 2001, I have had the privilege of being the dumbest person on an extremely smart team. Kerrick Thomas, Tommy Duke and Jason Hatley, in particular, have greatly shaped the thoughts in this book. To all of our current staff, I love doing church with you! To those whom God will call to our staff in the future, I look forward to being on the team with you. We having openings right now—get in touch!

I must also express my thanks to the now 2,100+ pastors who have completed one of my Senior Pastors Coaching Networks and the 1,000 founding members of The Renegade Pastors Network. Many of the ideas shared in these pages were first beta-tested on you. Your feedback, insights and improvements have made this a much stronger system. Thank you for living out the Learn and Return Principle.

Thanks are also due to my Advanced Coaching Network for providing the testimonies for each chapter and to Tommy Duke for the Scripture study guide at the end of this book. Thank you for making *The Renegade Pastor* stronger and more beneficial.

Jennifer Dykes Henson has been a partner on my last 10 books. Her commitment to the local church, communication and the ministry of writing never ends. This book was produced on our shortest timeline ever. And even though she was 6 minutes late with the final manuscript (yes, I'm bringing that up again—ha!), she continues to amaze me with her skill, energy and passion. Thank you, Jennifer! As members at The Journey, Jennifer and her husband, Brian, (and the hundreds of other couples like them at our church) make it a joy for me to fulfill my calling.

Even when I was writing for other publishers, Bill Greig III continued to be an ever-present source of advice, friendship and encouragement. He and Stan Jantz were the incubators for this project (and their skills of persuasion are evident, as they convinced

me to write the book on such a short deadline). Thank you, Bill, Stan, Kim Bangs and everyone on the team, for working with me again.

I must also thank the love of my life, Kelley. Unlike some spouses, Kelley knew she was marrying a "preacher," as I was already in ministry when we met. (In fact, she first saw me at a local church where I was a guest speaker. I've never dared to ask her if the sermon was any good.) One of my wise pastor friends told me upon our engagement, "A good spouse will double your ministry effectiveness." That has been an understatement in our marriage. Kelley has sacrificed, supported, encouraged, prodded, protected and fought for our ministry. Kelley, I love you now more than ever!

Finally, to my son, Alexander, who will turn seven years old just prior to the release of this book. I asked him last night what he wanted me to share with you. He said, "Tell them that I'm reading at one level higher than my grade." I'm a proud father! He then asked me if I included anything in the book about John the Baptist (that was his lesson on Sunday in Journey Kidz). Alexander, I pray for you every day—for you to grow in wisdom, in stature, in favor with men and in favor with God. (Me: Alex, I'm going to say goodnight now; I still have some writing to do. Alex: Aww, nuts!)

Thank you, Kelley and Alexander, for your commitment to this book, your continued support and your unconditional love.

From Jennifer Dykes Henson:

Thank you, first and always, to Jesus Christ for His unending love, amazing grace, and the incredible opportunity to be involved in His work on a daily basis.

I've always had an aversion to average, so being part of this book has been pure joy for me. I am humbled by and thankful for the opportunity to partner with Nelson in helping pastors reclaim their original passion for godly excellence through these pages. Thank you, Nelson, for inviting me into such life-changing work once again. Each successive book is more fun than the last.

Without the influence of my wonderful husband, Brian, I might never move from behind my computer screen. Brian, thank you for living (or should I say, enduring) the writer's life with me—and for making every new day an adventure.

# *Preface*

Excellence is an art won by training and habituation. We do not act
rightly because we have virtue or excellence, but we rather have
those because we have acted rightly. We are what we repeatedly
do. Excellence, then, is not an act but a habit.

ARISTOTLE

Now all glory to God, who is able, through his mighty
power at work within us, to accomplish infinitely
more than we might ask or think.

PAUL (EPHESIANS 3:20)

Why are you in ministry? What started you down this road in the
first place? My guess is that you felt called to accomplish great things
for God. You had a vision for reaching hurting people and introducing them to renewed life. You wanted to grow a healthy church that
would influence your community and draw people in to learn the
truth of the gospel. I bet you saw yourself setting your world on fire,
while leading a faithful family, having time to invest in your own
personal growth, and still finding enough free hours in the week to
enjoy life. So I have a question for you: How are you doing? Does
your current reality match the vision you had when you began living
the pastor's life?

If you are like the majority of pastors in the United States and
around the world, your years of ministry—whether 3 or 30—have
dialed your passion down a notch and your frustration up two. In the

midst of life's chaos and the pressures of doing church week to week, the verve you once had for godly excellence can subtly start taking a back seat to just getting by. Before you know it, you've settled for being average—an average leader leading an average church. But average is not what you've been called to.

## Trading Mediocrity for Meaning

Even though the pull of average is strong (you'll see just how strong in the Introduction to this book), there is a way to overcome it and step back toward a life of impact and excellence. If you are ready to break the bonds of lackluster living and get back to the business of putting a dent in hell, then read on. These pages are a guide for you and other leaders like you—leaders who want more; leaders who are ready to step up and stand in the tradition of Peter, Paul, James, Charles Spurgeon, Billy Sunday, C. S. Lewis, and other great, paradigm-challenging Christian leaders throughout history.

The topics covered in these pages are designed to help you move from mediocrity to meaning in every area of your life. You'll have the opportunity to explore many issues of personal and professional growth, such as:

- Managing your stress level
- Controlling your emotions
- Dealing with criticism
- Setting godly boundaries
- Being proactive with your time
- Becoming a better spouse and parent
- Establishing healthy friendships
- Developing strong church systems
- Personally honoring the Sabbath
- Planning with purpose
- And more

First, here are a few suggestions for how to get the most out of what's ahead:

1. *Read, question and digest this book.* Grab your favorite pen and work your way through the following pages. Make notes in the margins, disagree with me, laugh at me or raise your eyebrows. I don't mind. All I ask is that you move through the material thoroughly and with an open heart toward what God wants to accomplish in you and through you as you commit yourself to leaving the status quo in the dust and pursuing excellence in every area.

2. *Study this book with other pastors who want more.* Iron sharpens iron. As you work through the challenging and often contrarian ideas in these pages, you will benefit from being able to discuss them and begin embracing them with others who are tired of average too. Through this book, you and the other leaders around you can learn how to create an atmosphere of renegade thinking (more on that to come) as you help one another implement the principles I'll be detailing.

3. *Be open to new ideas.* Much of what you're about to encounter goes against traditional thinking. After all, traditional thinking is what has left so many pastors exasperated and so much of the church ineffective. If you run into an idea that is contrary to what you've been exposed to, that's okay. Stay open. Don't let the discomfort close your mind. I challenge accepted thinking, but never Scripture essentials.

4. *Visit this book's website, www.RenegadePastorBook.com.* I have created a website packed with free supplemental material to support what you will be learning through

these pages. As you begin to engage with the ideas here, make sure you visit www.RenegadePastorBook.com. Not only will you be able to connect with me and access a ton of useful renegade resources, but you'll also find detailed information on how you can become eligible to join the official Renegade Pastors Network.

As you set out on this adventure, I challenge you to listen to what God wants to say to you. Be honest about where you are in your personal life and where your church is, as compared to God's vision for both. Then have the courage to embrace the core commitments detailed ahead; they have the power to turn your frustration down and your passion back up, as they transform your life and your ministry from average to . . . renegade!

# *Abandoning Average:*
# A Tale of Two Pastors

Why diminish your soul being run-of-the-mill at something?
Mediocrity: now there is ugliness for you. Mediocrity's a
hairball coughed up on the Persian carpet of Creation.
TOM ROBBINS

I have come that they may have life, and have it to the full.
JESUS (JOHN 10:10, *NIV*)

Average. Mediocre. Run-of-the-mill. Those aren't terms you would want applied to your life or your work, are they? In fact, I bet they diametrically oppose the fire you had in your heart when you were called into ministry. "Average?" you would have said to me had I known you back then. "Who wants to be average? I am called to do God's work. I am going to change the world!" And I'm sure you set out to do just that. Fueled by sheer zeal and a God-given vision, your story began.

Have you checked in with your original enthusiasm lately? Are you still in the business of changing the world, or have you somehow slipped into maintenance mode? Are you still passionately abandoned for God, or has that fire dimmed beneath the pressure to get your message ready for the weekend, meet the budget, find people who are willing to volunteer, make it to your kid's Little League game, and be home in time for dinner? Even though you wouldn't want to admit any association with average thinking or mediocrity,

you may have felt their subtle pull. They tiptoe in and whisper to you through your frustration, your uncertainty and your lack of time. Before you know it, they have you shifting away from your pursuit of excellence for God's glory, focusing you instead on doing what it takes to get by from day to day.

The lives of two great pastors I know provide a perfect case study for the digression that so often happens in ministry. Alex and Rob are both faithful, well-intentioned guys. To a point, their lives were on similar trajectories. They were both called into ministry during college and went on to attend comparable seminaries. Now each of them pastors a mid-sized church in the Midwest. Like you, both Alex and Rob started out in ministry with grand visions of what the future would bring. Each of them wanted to influence lives and grow the Kingdom. Over the years, however, Alex's and Rob's paths have diverged. These days, they find themselves in strikingly different situations.

While Alex is frustrated with the lack of momentum in his church, the ever-present strain in his personal relationships, and his constant position behind the eight ball, Rob doesn't struggle in the same ways. His church is healthy and flourishing. He has quality relationships with the people close to him. Alex feels pressed by the clock every week, but Rob is able to handle the details and responsibilities of his work well and without too much stress. He even has time to set and work on personal goals that allow him to keep improving.

Both Alex and Rob have a strong work ethic and both are devoted to God's purposes for their lives, but Alex is slowly slipping deeper and deeper into a state of mediocrity, while Rob is growing and excelling in his life and ministry. What's the difference? Maybe the pseudo-last names I've given them for the purposes of this case study can be a clue: Alex Average allows daily circumstances and pressures to move him toward status-quo thinking, while Rob Renegade takes intentional steps to keep himself and his church healthy and thriving. These two mindsets, and the respective commitments Alex and Rob make to support them, are what separate the men; they are what separate every average pastor from every renegade pastor.

## Average vs. Renegade

Alex didn't intend to end up in the position he's in. He didn't start out in ministry thinking, *You know, my goal is to do average things with average people in an average way.* I bet you didn't either. If you can relate to where Alex is now, it's not because you want to be there. But despite your lofty visions and goals, the unrelenting pull of average is real and powerful. There is a daily, weekly, monthly grind that breeds mediocrity over time. Resistance is a live, active force.

Stephen Pressfield, author of *Do the Work* and *The War of Art*, writes at length about the nature of the agency he calls Resistance. Take a look at a couple of his observations:

> Resistance cannot be seen, heard, touched, or smelled. But it can be felt. . . . The more important a call or action is to our soul's evolution, the more Resistance we will feel toward pursuing it. . . . Resistance's goal is not to wound or disable. Resistance aims to kill. Its target is the epicenter of our being: our genius, our soul, the unique and priceless gift we were put on this earth to give.[1]

Pressfield's words sound a lot like Jesus' description, as recorded by John, of the devil himself: "The thief's purpose is to steal and kill and destroy" (John 10:10).

The enemy of your soul is also the enemy of the purposes God has for you on this earth. The devil wants nothing more than to thwart your ministry and derail your life. While he destroys some through major moral failures and unaddressed sin, one of his most dangerous tools is the subtle, unrelenting resistance he rains down on you in an attempt to get you to settle for average; for something on par with what everyone else is doing; for a life that's lacking the abundance Jesus came to give you; for a ministry that isn't operating anywhere near the redemptive potential that God has planned for it. He is an expert at using subtleties to sabotage. But as James says so plainly: "Resist the devil, and he will flee from you" (Jas. 4:7).

When you understand the state of the average church and the personal well-being of the average pastor, it's not hard to see why the devil wants you to be average. Attendance at the average church is declining by 9 percent every year. Nine percent is a dangerous number—just small enough that you don't notice it at first. By the time you do notice, you're already in trouble. That 9 percent drop in attendance generally equates to a 15 to 20 percent dip in the budget, which the average church is constantly behind on anyway.

Because it's always under financial strain, the average church isn't free to say yes to the ministry opportunities God brings its way. There's a culture of constant need and begging, for both money and volunteers. The average church begins a search for a new pastor every 18 months. Sometimes finding a new pastor is easier than dealing with the underlying problems that keep the church caught in the cycle of mediocrity. But a new pastor never solves the problem for long, because the average church has inadvertently put systems in place to keep both itself and its pastor average.

Like Alex, the average pastor is not managing his time well. A recent study showed that the typical pastor gets to work on Monday morning with no real plan for how the week should unfold. As a result, he spends his time reacting and responding to whatever pops up, rather than taking a proactive leadership role in the direction and health of his church. The average pastor operates in a state of silent desperation. His relationships are strained because he doesn't have adequate time to invest in them. Worst of all, he's not experiencing the fulfillment that should come from the calling God has placed on his life.

---

### The Average Pastor

#### Church:
- Attendance declining by 9% every year
- Always behind on budget
- Lacking sufficient volunteers
- Seeking new pastor every 18 months
- Unable to say yes to God's purposes

**Personally:**

- Frustrated
- Short on time
- Lives a reactive life
- Has strained relationships with family and friends
- Not experiencing fulfillment

Given these realities, do you think God has any desire for you to be average? Do you think He's happy with the level of your life and your work simply because you are doing no worse than the guys down the street? God has called you to more than mediocrity. He has called you to look to Him, to work as unto Him, to reflect His excellence, and to demonstrate His glory in a way that draws people in. You carry the awesome responsibility of introducing people to the Savior and discipling them to be more like Him. When it comes to that task, average doesn't cut it. Average doesn't lead to life change. Average is where the enemy wants you to live, because it is the precursor of ineffectiveness—but average is exactly what God is calling you to abandon.

One truth I've seen illustrated time and time again in consulting with wonderful, wonderfully frustrated pastors is that faithfulness and fruitfulness are not the same thing. Even if your heart is in the right place and your theology is solid—as is the case with most pastors—gaps in methodology and implementation still have the potential to derail your efforts. You can be the most faithful, God-fearing leader around and yet lead a dying church and have a troubled personal life if you aren't making the right decisions and implementing the right principles for the health of both. To be able to make those decisions and implement those principles, you simply need the knowledge, the tools and a few role models along the way.

 Faithfulness and fruitfulness are not the same thing.

In his classic spoken-word recording, *Lead the Field*, Earl Nightingale said, "If you want to be successful in life and you have no role models, look at what the majority of people are doing and do the opposite. The majority is always wrong."[2] When it comes to being a pastor, I couldn't agree more. If you want to grow a healthy church and have a happy personal life, one of the best things you can do is to look at what the majority of pastors are doing and do the opposite. In other words, decide to go renegade.

What exactly is a renegade pastor? A renegade is someone who has abandoned average in favor of excellence. He is a rebel with a purpose—someone who rises up against resistance, mediocrity and conformity. A renegade is not a lawbreaker. He is not contrarian for contrarianism's sake. He's not looking for a fight with other church leaders, but with the devil himself. He's not critical or cynical, but analytical in his thinking about what works in life and ministry and what doesn't. A renegade pastor is obedient to the Word of God and passionately abandoned for the Kingdom. He has made a decision to step out of the status quo and get back to the business of reflecting God's glory in every aspect of his life.

> If you want to grow a healthy church and have a happy personal life, look at what the average pastor is doing and do the opposite.

On an individual level, the renegade pastor is someone who lives in a state of faithful pro-activity. As Rob's story demonstrates, the renegade's church is healthy and growing; people are meeting Jesus and going deeper in their faith. The renegade pastor is a hard worker, but he knows how to work efficiently and manage his time for maximum benefit. He has quality relationships with his spouse, his children and his close friends; they don't feel cheated by the church. A renegade understands the importance of personal growth, so he is always learning. He knows how to identify godly goals and pursue them. And, unlike the average pastor, the renegade has peace about

his life and his work. He experiences the fulfillment that comes with the role God has called him to.

## The Renegade Pastor

### Defining Characteristics:

- Abandons average
- Challenges status quo thinking
- Obedient to God
- Rebels against resistance and mediocrity
- Contrarian for Kingdom purposes
- Student of what works and what doesn't work in life and ministry
- Passionately abandoned to the plans of God

### Additional Qualities:

- Pastors a healthy, growing church
- Enjoys authentic relationships with family and friends
- Dedicates time to personal and professional growth
- Lives a proactive life
- Experiences fulfillment in life and ministry

The differences between an average pastor and a renegade pastor are strikingly clear, so the question becomes: How do you bridge the divide between the two? What can you do to develop a life and ministry that look less like Alex's and more like Rob's? The answer lies in the commitments you choose to make.

## Character. Commitment. Discipline.

As a teenager, I spent some time traveling and speaking at young entrepreneur conferences around the country. Thanks to that circuit, I had the privilege of working alongside the late Zig Ziglar. A great businessman and leader, Zig spoke eloquently about matters of

vision, change, work and commitment. One statement Zig used to make often that has stuck with me through the years is this: "It's character that got us out of bed, commitment that moved us to action, and discipline that enabled us to follow through."

Character, commitment and discipline—the ability to move from where you are to where you want to be will flow from these three things. All intentional change is birthed out of character, anchored in the commitments you make, and executed through discipline. Your character drove you to pick up this book, because something within you is longing to take your life and ministry up a notch—to the level where you know it should be. Perhaps you can feel average tugging at your shirtsleeve, and you know it's leading you toward a trap to be avoided at all costs.

Discipline will determine how well you follow through with the adjustments you want to make. In the pages ahead, I will give you the knowledge and tools you need to begin living like a renegade, but how effectively you apply them to your life is in your hands. I can guarantee, though, that if you make a decision to raise your game for God's glory, He will meet you where you are and help you move to where He wants you to be.

That leaves the issue of commitments. Your life is shaped by the commitments you choose to make. If you look back through your past, I'm sure you can identify a handful of commitments that have had a major impact on where you are today. You made a commitment to surrender your life to God and follow Him into the work of ministry. Maybe you made a commitment to go to one particular school over another, and that has put you on your current trajectory. You may have made the commitment to share your life with a spouse, or you may still be hoping to make that commitment one day. If you have children, you have made a commitment to care for them and raise them well. Each one of these is a life-changing decision.

 The commitments you make determine the direction of your life.

The commitments you make determine the direction of your life. They define you. As you refine your commitments, you shape the contours of your future. When it comes to abandoning average and beginning to live the no-holds-barred life of a renegade, there are seven essential commitments you must make in order to put and keep yourself on the right path. You already possess the character. By making these seven commitments—and then having the discipline to follow through with them—you can leave mediocrity behind for good and move toward the excellence and impact you are called to.

## The Seven Commitments of a Renegade Pastor

In the chapters ahead, I'll break down each of these seven commitments and explore them in detail, but here is a quick overview:

### Commitment One—Follow Your Lord

Properly aligned priorities are critical to your success as a pastor, a spouse, a parent, a friend and an individual. But here's the thing with priorities: It's easy to say they are one thing and live as if they are another. Is seeking after God your number one priority in truth or just in word? What is your second priority? You may be surprised by what it should be. There are specific steps you can take to make sure your priorities are aligned correctly and to keep them that way—and to ensure that being busy with God's work doesn't crowd out the work He wants to do in you.

### Commitment Two—Love Your Family

Are you afraid your ministry work will destroy your marriage? Or keep your kids from growing up to love the Lord? No pastor plans to find himself in a marital or family crisis, but too many end up there because they don't plan *not* to. Loving your family is not passive; you can't just hope that, since you are serving God, everything will work

out okay. Instead, by intentionally putting some specific boundaries and hedges in place to protect the relationships closest to you, you can show active love for your family while shielding them from some of the common pitfalls associated with ministry.

## Commitment Three — Fulfill Your Calling

When you were called into ministry, you didn't have everything you needed to fulfill your calling. You have gathered—and are still gathering—essential elements along the way. Are you collecting what you need to be successful, or are the tools you are putting in your tool belt only serving to keep you average?

## Commitment Four — Manage Your Time

If you are like most pastors, you are constantly behind the eight ball—running out of time to prepare for Sunday, to set up this or that ministry, to read the books on your list, or to invest quality hours with your family. Effective time management can revolutionize your life. Time is the most precious commodity you have. How are you spending it?

## Commitment Five — Shepherd Your Flock

There is a lot of uncertainty surrounding the best, most biblical way to shepherd the people in your care. It's time to demystify the role of the shepherd so that you can step into proper leadership and disciple your people the way God intends. After all, one day you'll be held accountable for how well you've done the job.

## Commitment Six — Maximize Your Church

What does the full redemptive potential of your church look like? Are you doing all you can to cooperate with God in structuring your church for maximum impact on this earth? God wants your church to be healthy and flourishing, and there are specific steps you can take to help it get there.

## Commitment Seven — Expand God's Kingdom

Sometimes it is so easy to get busy with day-to-day ministry concerns that you lose perspective on your position within the bigger picture.

There's tremendous value in keeping an eye turned toward new church plants, missions work, and the other opportunities you have to engage in the overall growth of God's kingdom.

At first glance, these commitments may not seem all that renegade, but I have a feeling you'll be surprised by just how unconventional they really are. Beneath the surface, the details of these commitments and their supporting principles are revolutionary. They have the potential to transform your life and ministry from average into an ongoing illustration of God's excellence.

## The Original Renegade

Take another look at the two charts detailing the differences between an average pastor and a renegade pastor:

### *The Average Pastor*

#### Church:
- Attendance declining by 9% every year
- Always behind on budget
- Lacking sufficient volunteers
- Seeking new pastor every 18 months
- Unable to say yes to God's purposes

#### Personally:
- Frustrated
- Short on time
- Lives a reactive life
- Has strained relationships with family and friends
- Not experiencing fulfillment

### The Renegade Pastor

**Defining Characteristics:**

- Abandons average
- Challenges status quo thinking
- Obedient to God
- Rebels against resistance and mediocrity
- Contrarian for Kingdom purposes
- Student of what works and what doesn't work in life and ministry
- Passionately abandoned to the plans of God

**Additional Qualities:**

- Pastors a healthy, growing church
- Enjoys authentic relationships with family and friends
- Dedicates time to personal and professional growth
- Lives a proactive life
- Experiences fulfillment in life and ministry

Now, let me ask you: Which description sounds more like Jesus? Would you characterize Him as an average guy doing average things, or as a trailblazer set on changing the world for God's glory? The question seems ludicrous, doesn't it?

Jesus was constantly challenging the standard thinking of His day and calling people to passion, purpose and excellence. He disrupted accepted religious thought and was often contrarian with Kingdom purposes. The defining characteristics of a renegade pastor parallel Jesus' life and ministry perfectly. There was no room for settling or status quo thinking in His life. In fact, Jesus was the original renegade.

As the original renegade, Jesus wants nothing less from you—you can be sure of that. As He says Himself, "I tell you the truth, anyone who believes in me will *do the same works I have done, and even greater works*, because I am going to be with the Father" (John 14:12, emphasis added).

The days of average are over. A new level of living is calling your name. God wants to put you back on the path toward the original vision He placed in your heart when He called you into ministry. Even more, He wants to do greater things in you and through you than you've ever imagined possible (see Eph. 3:20). The next move is yours. Are you ready to go renegade?

# *Commitment One:*
# Follow Your Lord

*Doing the Work of God Without Destroying God's Work in You*

You cannot be a leader, and ask other people to
follow you, unless you know how to follow, too.
SAM RAYBURN

Come, follow me.
JESUS (MARK 1:17)

Not long ago, my wife, Kelley, and I had the opportunity to spend
a few days in Rome. We decided to get our bearings on the first day
by joining a guide-led walking tour of the city. As the tour began,
Kelley and I were determined to stay right behind our guide, Chris,
so that we could hear everything he said. But if you have ever been
on a large walking tour in a major metropolis, you know how hard
that can be. If you pause for even a second to take a picture or
admire some marvel of architecture, you fall back. Suddenly there
are people, conversations and city noises wedged between you and
your guide.

That's exactly what happened to us. We spent a little too much
time taking in Bernini's sculpture at the base of the obelisk in Piazza
Navona (if you haven't seen it, put it on your list), and when we turned
back toward the group, we realized they had moved on. It only took

us a minute to catch up, but we found ourselves at the back of the tour—so far away from Chris that we couldn't hear exactly what he was saying. Sure, we still caught snippets of his explanations here and there, but because we had let so many people and distractions move in between us, we had lost our connection with him. Even though we saw a lot of interesting things during the rest of the tour, we weren't sure exactly what context they fit into or why they were significant.

If Kelley and I had stayed in step with Chris throughout the tour, we would have gotten a lot more of the insight we needed to make the most of our time in Rome. In addition, we would have been able to help the people behind us by passing along information to them that they couldn't hear for themselves. Getting separated from our leader not only limited our own experience, but also disqualified us from serving anyone else.

## Follow the Leader

That experience with Chris got me thinking about what it means to be a good follower—especially when it comes to following the real Leader in my life. I had to ask myself if I ever let distractions, other people and everyday demands wedge themselves between Jesus and me. Then I had to admit that I have. Have you? Have you dropped back from Jesus' guidance for one reason or another and quickly found yourself too far away to make out His whispers? You may still be able to hear when He turns the volume up, but maybe you feel like you've lost your intimate, ongoing communion with Him. Following closely enough behind Jesus to hear what He's saying all the time is critical to your life and ministry. When you can't hear from Him clearly, you can't do His will. What's more, if you aren't being a good follower, you're not well equipped to lead.

 If you aren't being a good follower, you're not well equipped to lead.

If you look back through the Scriptures, it's easy to see that the strongest biblical leaders have always been the greatest followers. Abraham famously followed God to a place he knew nothing about, based on God's promises to him (see Gen. 12:1-3). Because of his willingness to abide with God so deeply, Abraham has been called a father of the faith. Every new generation throughout history has been able to learn from him and draw on his example. Moses, following God, led more than 600,000 people out of Egypt, in the middle of the night, on a journey toward the Promised Land (see Exod. 12:31-42). Because Moses was committed to following his Lord as he led others, future leaders like Joshua benefited from his faithfulness and were able to walk in his example.

Jesus Himself is the greatest example of authentic followership. Jesus' life was centered on the singular purpose of walking in step with and bringing glory to His Father. He called His disciples to do the same. As He identified the inner circle that would walk with Him, Jesus said simply, "Come, follow me" (Mark 1:17). He didn't say, "Take care of your family needs, make sure your business is in order, and then we'll talk." He said, "Follow." As the disciples made following the Son of God their top priority, their lives were transformed; they eventually became the leaders of the faith God intended for them to be. Through intimate, ongoing communion with Jesus, they were not only strengthened personally but also better equipped to minister to the countless others who would be entrusted to their leadership.

 ### Renegade Commitment One: Follow Your Lord

The first commitment of being a renegade pastor is to follow your Lord in the same way these great examples throughout history have—to make your communion with Him more important than anything else in your life. I can hear you pushing back already. You are probably thinking, *Come on, this is elementary. I'm a pastor. Of course I'm following the Lord.* Let me challenge you to leave the surface level and dive a little deeper. The question isn't *if* you are following;

it's *how closely* are you following? Your proximity to Jesus will define your life and leadership. Everything you do as a leader, a spouse, a parent, a mentor and a friend hinges on how good a follower you are.

There have likely been times in your life, as there have been in mine, when you've been so close to Jesus that you could hear His every whisper. There may have been other times when you've hung back. I encourage you to pause here for some honest self-evaluation: Right now, as you read these words, how intimate is your relationship with Jesus? How closely are you following Him, *really*? Are you right on His heels, positioned to hear every word that comes out of His mouth? Or are you distracted? Are you dropping back and allowing other people or things to come between you and Him? Your answers to these questions are directly linked to the current state of your life and ministry.

Too often, I hear stressed-out pastors complain that the demands of ministry keep them from following God like they want to—that the never-ending needs of church and family rob them of their intimate, personal connection with the Lord. Maybe you have felt that way. Maybe you have even said the same thing yourself. But here's the truth: The only way doing the work of God can destroy the work of God in you is if you let it. After all, you know that's not God's intention; He wants quite the opposite. Everything you do in ministry should flow from a deep place of strength as you continually follow God more and more closely. And it can. All you have to do is align your priorities the renegade way.

 The only way doing the work of God can destroy the work of God in you is if you let it.

## Shuffling Priorities

Don't you love how Christians come up with acronyms for everything? There's even one for how you should arrange your priorities in order to experience God's closeness and joy in your life. You've

probably come across it at some point. According to the acronym, joy comes as you put Jesus first, others second and yourself third. JOY. **J**esus. **O**thers. **Y**ourself. Sounds good, right? Sounds like a godly way to live. There's only one problem: The acronym is wrong.

The **J** is right, of course. Without question, your relationship with Jesus should be your number one priority. And it's true that joy is ultimately found through your connection with Him, not in your ever-changing circumstances. If you base your sense of joy, peace and contentment on what happens to you, you will wind up on an emotional roller-coaster ride. But if you remain grounded in the fact that you are an adopted child of God and a joint heir with Christ in the Kingdom, then your joy will be stable. As you continually seek Jesus and draw closer to Him, you'll be able to stand strong on the solid foundation of His promises no matter what is going on around you.

The **O** and the **Y**, on the other hand, have always bothered me. What this acronym misses is the interplay that happens between you and Jesus as you put Him first in your life. When you make Jesus your highest priority, He goes to work refining you so that you come to look more like Him. He starts growing you and maturing you into the fully developing follower He wants you to be. But to accomplish His purposes in you, He needs your cooperation. You have to stay right behind Him, listening for His voice and doing what He tells you to do. In order to keep that close, you need to put yourself, rather than others, in the second spot on your priority list. If you let other people move between you and Jesus, you run the very real risk of crowding out your connection with Him, drowning His voice, and thwarting the work He wants to do in you.

I know this thinking is contrarian. You have always been taught that the Christian thing to do is to put others before yourself. But while that expectation sounds pious in theory, it's actually a recipe for disaster. In working with countless pastors and other church leaders over the years, I have observed a major trend: The pressure to focus on everyone else's needs before concentrating on Jesus and

what He wants to do in you personally is the fastest way to crash and burn. Letting others direct your life causes emotional stress, robs you of your focus, disrupts your peace, and leads to continually diminishing returns in every area.

Now, don't get me wrong. I am not saying that servanthood shouldn't be one of the highest-ranking priorities of your life; it should be. You are called to be a servant, just as Jesus was. Jesus Himself says, "The greatest among you must be a servant" (Matt. 23:11).

But biblical servanthood doesn't mean sacrificing your connection with God and your own growth for others. There were times when even Jesus saw urgent problems around Him and chose not to meet them because He needed to spend time with the Father. He pulled away from the crowds to focus on what God wanted to do *in* Him, so that God could ultimately do what He wanted to do *through* Him. Look at Luke's account:

> The report of his power spread even faster, and vast crowds came to hear him preach and to be healed of their diseases. But Jesus often withdrew to the wilderness for prayer (Luke 5:15-16).

I spend a lot of time on airplanes. Every time the flight attendants go through the pre-flight safety instructions, I think about this truth. Without fail, they always give the same direction about what to do if cabin pressure drops and oxygen masks become necessary. You know what it is: *Be sure to secure your own mask before helping others.* Why? Because if you don't, you may lose consciousness yourself—and that would be bad for everyone. Of course no one would argue with the airlines' wisdom, yet in ministry the accepted rule seems to be to help everyone else first, even if it's at the expense of your own well-being—even if you are gasping for air and about to pass out. Can I get a witness?

Choosing to keep yourself healthy—spiritually, emotionally, mentally and physically—by staying constantly connected to the

source of your strength isn't selfish at all. Quite the opposite. Taking care of your relationship with Christ, and giving time to the ways He wants to grow you, is the very thing that equips you to serve your family and your ministry. Given that reality, consider arranging your priorities more like this:

- Jesus
- You
- Your Family
- Others

There's no catchy acronym for this new alignment, but there is power in its implementation. To arrange things any other way would be a disservice not only to Jesus, but also to yourself and to everyone who depends on you. Your strength, your growth, your peace and your joy come through your relationship with Christ.. Out of that, you become better able to serve the people around you. You become a leader who has the time, the wisdom and the reserves to take care of your responsibilities in every area without being stressed out or emotionally drained. Be careful not to lose this truth in the pseudo-spiritual demand to sacrifice yourself on the altar of others' needs.

## Renegade Pastor Testimony

Not too long ago, I became aware of a nagging emptiness within. I seemed to have lost my way in doing ministry. One day I was fine; the next I realized that doing ministry wasn't the same as spending time with Jesus. My soul had shriveled while I was busy being busy—busy doing what I thought was most important: ministry. But ministry and leadership did not and could not do for me what worship could. The practice of prayer, solitude, quietness and reading Scripture for myself has revived my soul. Getting back to the basics

has provided a breath of life to me personally. I'm a better pastor because of it.

Alan Allen, Senior Pastor
The Vineyard Church—Pearland, Texas

## Getting Practical

So what does it look like, practically speaking, to put Jesus first in your life and yourself second? Well, here's what it doesn't look like: It doesn't look like giving yourself a green light to do whatever pleases you rather than meeting the needs of others. This is in no way an invitation to self-indulgence or laziness. Instead, it's about making two intentional decisions about your priorities and then protecting those decisions:

*Decision #1:* Dedicate daily time to your personal fellowship with Jesus.

*Decision #2:* Dedicate daily time to growing yourself in the ways He leads you.

To gauge how well you are doing with these two prioritizations right now, consider these questions:

- At what time of day do you pull away to focus on your relationship with God?
- Is your day so fully scheduled with ministry and family demands that it's hard to find time to maintain your connection to Jesus or to let Him grow you?
- How often do you put time and energy into godly goal setting or into the training that could make you a better servant?

An overly packed schedule is a major obstacle to being able to hear from God. If you don't intentionally invest time in your relationship with Jesus, the other things clamoring for your attention

will get in the way. But when you make a decision to rightly align and protect your priorities, you will change the way you manage your time (read: your life), no matter what else is going on. Let me challenge you to carve out time every day to unapologetically focus on your relationship with God and on the things He wants to do in and through you. Here are four tips to help you get started:

## 1. Don't get hung up on the time of day.

In the church world, there's a lot of pressure to give your mornings to God. That is, to have your devotional and prayer time as soon as you wake up, before the distractions of the day come rolling in. While I do believe that morning devotionals are great if they work for you, everyone is different. If you aren't wired in a way that's conducive to an early morning quiet time, then it's perfectly acceptable to choose another time during the day to pull away and be still before God—as long as you do it. Yes, Jesus got up early to spend time with the Father, but He also went to bed when the sun went down. Electric lights usually keep you and me from doing that. There is nothing more holy about communing with God at 4:30 AM than there is about spending time with Him at 11:30 PM—or at any hour in between. You have to figure out what works for you.

Once you identify the best time of day for your one-on-one time with Jesus, protect that appointment. No matter where it falls, it is the most important chunk of time on your schedule. I can guarantee that when it's time for your quiet time, something will try to distract you; someone will try to crowd it out; an issue will pop up that seems to need your immediate attention. Don't bite. Protect your priority and unapologetically focus on your relationship with Jesus.

 An overly packed schedule is a major obstacle to being able to hear from God.

**2. Discuss your priorities with the people in your inner circle.**
The people closest to you need to know what your priorities are and that you want to be diligent about preserving them. They can help you keep those priorities from being ravaged by daily life. Not to mention, agreements on the front end prevent disagreements on the back end. If the people in your life understand your priorities, they won't feel slighted if those commitments sometimes interfere with their needs.

If you are married, have this conversation with your spouse. Make sure the two of you are on the same page. Kelley and I have an agreement: We each help the other to be a committed follower of the Lord. She gives me the space I need to spend time with God. She knows I can't be the man, father or pastor I am supposed to be without it. In the same way, I do whatever needs to be done to allow her to have her time with God. Honoring that priority makes her a better woman, a better spouse, a better mother and a better minister within our church. This way, even when the demands of family life start to seem overwhelming, we can help each other stay focused on what is most important: honoring our commitment to follow God and continuing to grow up in Him.

**3. Don't be shy about borrowing and adapting from others.**
Before I became a pastor, I was on an engineering track. The first rule of engineering is: "Don't reinvent the wheel." When I made the transition into ministry, I saw a lot of well-intentioned pastors driving themselves crazy doing just that. They were starting from scratch every single week, with everything from Sunday follow-up to sermon preparation and worship planning. As a result, not only did their time with God get pushed to the periphery, but they also had no time for personal growth, and their families felt neglected. Given my engineering mindset, I began designing systems, checklists and strategies to help these dedicated pastors better cooperate with God's plan for their churches week to week.

Over the years, these systems and strategies have become highly developed and refined. Pastors around the world borrow and adapt

them to fit their church environments, saving themselves the time, energy and stress of having to reinvent the wheel week in and week out. These pastors now lead healthier churches, without letting their time for God, family or their own personal development slide. They've learned the importance of working in conjunction with the systems and principles God put in place for His Church in order to be both more efficient and more effective. (For more on developing healthy church systems, see Chapter 6 and visit www.RenegadePastorBook.com.)

Learning to borrow and adapt what's already working for others is a much-overlooked necessity of ministry, particularly early on. For a new pastor, especially one who is bi-vocational, the demands of the church, on top of family and work, are often overwhelming. The pressure of having to come up with a fresh message every week can be the straw that breaks the camel's back, sending him into desperation. That's one reason I often encourage young pastors and church planters to borrow and adapt not just strategies but even specific messages from other people, especially in their first few years of ministry. Repurposing already preached sermons can lighten the load considerably—and there's nothing wrong with it.

If you don't like the idea of preaching from someone else's notes, keep in mind that the commentaries from one generation back were nothing but the sermons of the previous generation. It's only in recent years that commentaries have become all about Greek and Hebrew interpretations. Before that, they were simply a collection of sermons that preacher after preacher pulled into his own repertoire and tweaked. That's not stealing; it's just ministry. If another preacher's bullet fits your gun, take it and shoot it. Learn, borrow and adapt from those who have come before you, just as they did from those who came before them.

## 4. Delegate distractions.

A wise man once advised me to focus on my strengths and delegate my weaknesses. This effective principle can be applied to managing priorities. Sometimes time with God gets pushed out not by other

people's urgent needs or important ministry demands, but just by the mundane details of life.

For example, I recently coached a pastor who said to me, "I feel like I don't have time to spend with God, because every time I get a free minute, I come face to face with a honey-do list that's three pages long." You know what my advice was? Hire a handyman for $10 an hour who can take care of the honey-do list. Don't trade the important things in life for the urgent things in life. You have to learn to delegate the non-essentials if they are keeping you from being able to focus on what really is essential.

Let me emphasize again, this is not an excuse for being lazy. Delegating distractions is not code for getting out of home repair jobs, domestic chores or anything else, if you can do those things. But if busywork is crowding out your time to focus on God and what He wants to do through you, figure out how to get that busywork off of your plate. Put first things first.

## The Principle of the First

One of the most powerful principles in Scripture is something I like to refer to as *The Principle of the First*. According to the Principle of the First, God will bless the areas of your life where you put Him in first place. If you want God to bless your finances, put Him first in your finances. If you want Him to bless your family, put Him first in your family. If you want Him to bless your ministry, put Him first in your ministry. First equals blessing. As you can see, Commitment One of being a renegade pastor flows directly from the Principle of the First. Following your Lord closely hinges on putting Him first in every area of your life—not just in word but also in truth.

 *The Principle of the First*: God will bless the areas of your life where you put Him in first place.

Your life and your ministry will be defined by how well you follow your Lord. In the same way that Kelley and I couldn't hear

what Chris was saying when we dropped back and allowed others to move between us and him, so too you won't be able to hear the whispers of Jesus unless you commit to following right on His heels. When you choose to make Him your number one priority and the work He wants to do in you your second priority, you will begin going deeper as a disciple than you ever knew was possible. You will be better able to reflect His excellence to the world. And you will be better equipped to love and serve those around you, saying to them as Paul said to the church at Corinth: "Be imitators of me, just as I also am of Christ" (1 Cor. 11:1, *NASB*).

### *Renegade Pastor Testimony*

Being a renegade pastor has reinvigorated my relationship with Jesus. Consequently it has revitalized my priorities. I've come to believe that my time is more valuable than money. I'm now using this most precious resource to live out kingdom values and serve others for eternity. I'm proud to be a renegade pastor.

Jeff Warner, Senior Pastor
MCF Community Church—College Park, Maryland

# *Commitment Two:* Love Your Family

*Refusing to Sacrifice Your Family on the Altar of Ministry*

A man ought to live so that everybody knows he is a Christian . . .
and most of all, his family ought to know.
D. L. MOODY

But from everlasting to everlasting the LORD's love is with those
who fear him, and his righteousness with their children's children.
DAVID (PSALM 103:17, *NIV*)

Have you ever counseled engaged or newlywed couples? Their naïveté is captivating. In their minds, love is all rainbows and butterflies. Even the hint that staying in love and protecting their future family will require commitment and intentional decision-making is usually met with shock. They wonder, incredulously, how they could ever be anything but madly in love and devoted to making each other a high priority? What these young couples fail to realize is that, despite their current level of infatuation, love is much more than the feelings they're experiencing. At its core, love is a verb—an action verb—and how well they put that verb into action in relation to their family will not only determine their future happiness but also largely define their life and legacy.

It's easy to understand this truth when looking at other couples, but things get trickier when the light shines toward you and me. Let me put you on the spot: How much do you love your family? I'm not talking about a passive, feelings-based love, but about a love that is active and engaged—a love that truly honors the Lord you are following. Consider the question this way: How intentional are the decisions you make about your family life? Do the concerns of ministry crowd out time and energy that should be focused on your spouse and children?

You would be surprised just how often desperate, well-meaning pastors tell me that they are so overwhelmed with church concerns that they are neglecting not only their relationship with God (as discussed in the last chapter) but also their relationship with their family. They can see the cracks starting to appear, but they don't know what to do to change things. As a result, they go about their days terrified that they are sacrificing their marriage and their children's well-being on the altar of ministry, and praying that God will hold everything together. In reality, busyness and ministry demands are not to blame here; the real culprits are disorganization and a lack of intentionality.

 No pastor plans to find himself in a marital or family crisis, but too many end up there because they don't plan *not* to.

Do you have safety measures in place to protect your relationships with your family members? Do you have a strategy for safeguarding your personal and family integrity? No pastor plans to find himself in a marital or parenting crisis, but too many end up there because they don't plan *not* to. The decisions you make and the actions you take concerning your family today are the building blocks of the relationships you are going to have—or not have—with your loved ones in years to come.

No doubt, you've heard the same tragic stories I have through the years—stories of pastors having illicit affairs, living secret lives, and destroying their families in the same ways and at the same rate

(according to some studies, at a higher rate) as non-Christians. I'm sure you also know of less severe but no less dangerous tales of pastors whose families suffer because of the discrepancies between the life lived inside the church and the one lived at home. You've likely met pastors whose spouses feel like ministry widows because there is no equilibrium between church commitments and family time, and whose kids act out in shocking ways due to a lack of grounding and balance. These accounts are so common they've become cliché, not to mention a sad joke to unbelieving onlookers.

If the way you manage your home mirrors the way everyone else manages theirs, you will find yourself dealing with the same average (read: tragic) results, in one form or another. But with a little intentionality, you can keep your spouse and children from being sacrificed on the altar of ministry. Average pastors put their marriage and family life on autopilot, hoping that, because they are called to God's work, everything will stay on track through the years—but not doing a lot to ensure that outcome. They love their families, of course, but passively and without much concern for the long-term effects of daily decisions. On the other hand, renegades, recognizing that love is more than a feeling, make a conscious decision to love their spouse and children with intention. They actively latch onto the second commitment that defines the renegade life: Love your family.

 ### Renegade Commitment Two: Love Your Family

What does this active love look like? How can you intentionally love your family in a way that creates an authentic, happy home environment? How can you grow your relationship with your spouse into the deep, intimate partnership it should be? How can you invest in your children and raise them in a way that leads to their seeking after God and His will for their lives? The way you choose to address questions like these is the true measure of how much you love your family. All renegade-worthy answers fall under the canopy of three important concepts: (1) boundaries, (2) hedges, and (3) hard work.

By putting these three principles into action, you'll be able to love your family in a way that gives you the best opportunity to deepen your relationships, protect your integrity, and leave a lasting legacy for your children and your children's children after them.

## Boundaries

There's a lot to be said for dorm living during the college years. The community atmosphere is good for most kids at that time in life, especially if they have decent roommates. Unfortunately, one of my closest friends, James, didn't have such a great dorm experience. During his sophomore year, he was assigned a roommate who turned out to be a disaster. James would often come back to his dorm after class and find his roommate's clothes strewn across both sides of the room. The roommate would use James's desk because his own was so cluttered, usually leaving drinks and half-eaten snacks behind. Even though the room was supposed to be an equally divided space, the roommate lived like the whole place belonged to him. There were no boundaries.

One day, while his nemesis was in class, James bought a large roll of duct tape and used it to mark out a boundary line down the middle of the room. When his roommate got back, James told him that if he or his things crossed that line, there was going to be a penalty to pay. (I don't know exactly what the penalty would have been, but James was a pretty big guy; I wouldn't have wanted to test him.) Though not the most original idea in the world, the line down the center of the room was effective. Mr. Messy got the message and started keeping himself and his stuff on his side. The rest of the school year went smoothly, and the following year James applied for a single room.

 You can keep your spouse and children from being sacrificed on the altar of ministry.

Boundaries are simply guidelines to indicate where one thing ends and something else begins. They can be thought of as rules you put

in place to safeguard and deepen the relationships that exist within them. One of the single best ways to love your family intentionally is to set up boundaries between various areas of your life. For example, defining the boundary between ministry life and family life is key to creating a happy home. What falls on the ministry side of the boundary is another discussion for another time. For now, I want you to begin thinking about what it looks like to draw a boundary line around your home life, in order to protect and nurture what's inside.

## Get Out the Duct Tape

What are the pressure points that you are constantly running into with your spouse or your children? Those are generally good indicators of where you need to lay down some boundary lines. Think about something that frustrates you and your family, then back off of that frustration and ask yourself what kind of boundary could eliminate it. For example, if your spouse is frustrated that you always have your phone in your hand—texting, emailing, talking or whatever you are doing—when your attention should be on the family, create a boundary to alleviate that frustration. Here are some possible guidelines that could do the trick:

- Decide to put your phone away between the time you get home for dinner and when the kids go to bed.
- Set a "no cell phones at the dinner table" rule for you, your spouse and your kids. This boundary alone can go a long way toward connecting you with your family on a daily basis.
- Set a "phone off" time every night and stick to it. Once your phone is off, put it out of sight until the next morning.

One frustration Kelley and I used to run into is that I was consistently late getting home for dinner. After several years of unnecessary head butting, I realized that I kept breaking myself against this boundary between ministry and home because I had drawn too strict a line. I just needed to cushion it a little. Let me explain:

Say Kelley checks in with me around 5:30 PM to see what time I'm going to be home. I used to mentally take out my duct tape and mark my boundary as close to the ministry side of things as possible. For example, my internal monologue went something like this: *Okay, I've got about 15 minutes of work left to do. If I rush, I can probably do it in 10 minutes. Then, if I make the light out of the office park and there's not a lot of traffic, I could probably be home at 6:00.* So I would give the best-case scenario and say 6:00. As a result, even if I finished my work quickly and made great time getting home, but walked in at 6:10, I was late.

 Think about something that frustrates you and your family, then back off of that frustration and ask yourself what kind of boundary could eliminate it.

Now I've learned to make that boundary line a little more comfortable by giving Kelley the worst-case scenario. Given the same circumstances as above, I would tell her that I'd be home at 6:15 or 6:20 instead of 6:00. She doesn't care what the time is as long as I'm home when I say I'm going to be there. Thanks to the new boundary line, I would have plenty of time to finish up my work, even deal with some slow traffic, and still make it home on time, if not a few minutes early. Then I'm the hero. I am showing respect for my family by being on time and ready to focus on them. This one small tweak helped to create harmony in my home.

Think through the boundaries you already have in place and consider the ones you may need to set up. Do you allow television during dinner? Do you commit to taking a certain amount of family vacation time annually? Have you put a boundary around your Sabbath to keep it holy? (More on the power of honoring the Sabbath in Chapter 4.) Do you and your spouse plan time to get away alone?

Speaking of getting away with your spouse: I suggest putting a big boundary in place around date night. Having a regularly scheduled evening of one-on-one time with your spouse is paramount to keeping

your relationship healthy. Given your current situation, you may only be able to schedule a date night once a month. If you can, I highly recommend making it once a week. Whatever you decide you can do, put those nights on your calendar and secure the boundary lines around them. Don't let ministry concerns or anything else encroach on them.

From time to time pastors will say to me, "I like the idea of date night but I can't afford it," and/or, "Who will watch the kids?" Date nights don't have to be expensive. Every once in a while, you may want to do something special that costs some money—maybe for an anniversary or a birthday—but there are lots of ways to have romantic dates on a regular basis without stretching yourself financially. You could make a picnic and take it to a local park. Talk about what God is doing in your lives and family while you eat your packed sandwiches. Or stay home, order a pizza and pop in a movie. As far as the kids go, try trading date nights with another couple. Watch their kids so they can go out (or stay in) for an evening and then vice versa. Be creative. Don't let excuses—or a lack of boundary setting—push out what's most important.

Where would boundaries help you solve a problem or eliminate a recurring frustration? Take this principle and apply it to whatever needs correcting or protecting in your life. Wherever your boundary lines need to be, mark them out thoughtfully—and then honor them once they're in place.

## Stepping Over the Line

As you begin laying down the imaginary duct tape, think about how you step across that line as you leave one zone and enter another. In other words, what does your transition time between work and home look like? Even if you have great boundaries set up at home, you have to know how to decompress during the time between when you step away from the work atmosphere and when you enter into the family atmosphere. Keeping boundaries becomes difficult if you don't transition well between zones. I'm sure you know this from personal experience. For example, if you leave something unfinished

at the church to rush home for dinner, it's hard to make the mental shift that will allow you to honor the boundaries you've set. You can easily end up sitting at the dinner table, mentally consumed by what you were working on an hour earlier.

 Keeping boundaries becomes difficult if you don't transition well between zones.

Figuring out what best helps you transition from work to home will be a personal journey, but here are a few effective tactics I've seen used: One pastor I worked with would always make himself a cup of coffee on the way out the door. The simple act of drinking a cup of coffee on the way home helped him transition out of the workday and into family mode. Another guy I know used to give himself 30 extra minutes between leaving work and getting home. He would go sit in a park just down the street from his office and put together his to-do list for the next day. That helped him clear his mind so he could be present with his family when he got home.

I once heard Zig Ziglar say that when he arrived home from a speaking engagement, he would circle the block one time before pulling into his driveway. That minute or two that he took to drive around his block was his cue to transition out of work mode and into family mode. For you, it could be something as simple as a playlist you like to listen to on the way home. Or maybe it's taking 10 minutes before you leave your church or the office to think through how the day has played out and make a note of anything that didn't get done. Give your family this gift, in whatever way works best for you. When you get home, they want, need and deserve all of you.

### Renegade Pastor Testimony

Second only to my relationship with God is my family. In a growing church, maintaining this commitment can be a challenge. I am thankful for Nelson's encouragement to keep my

priorities God-honoring. I have seen so many pastors struggle in their marriages and have their kids end up resenting
the church. The principles I have learned about loving my
family have helped me make my marriage better than ever—
and both my boys love the church. All the while, we've had
six years of steady church growth. It is possible.

Michael Shreve, Pastor
Mountain West Church—Stone Mountain, Georgia

## Hedges

While boundaries are proactive rules you set to make sure things
work well internally, hedges are protective barriers you build to
keep out the onslaught of attacks that will inevitably come your
way. Boundaries exist to preserve and bolster what's within them;
hedges exist to keep the bad stuff—the poison, the negativity and
the temptation—at bay. Again, the devil would love to take you
down. He would love to drive you out of ministry and destroy your
family. As Peter writes, "Stay alert! Watch out for your great enemy,
the devil. He prowls around like a roaring lion, looking for someone
to devour" (1 Pet. 5:8).

Satan has many tactics in his derailment strategy for your life.
Being aware of his go-to weapons can help you stand against them.
Robert Clinton, the longtime professor of leadership at Fuller
Theological Seminary, created a list of the six most common down-
falls for pastors—or, as he phrased it, six barriers to finishing well.
I'll first give you the whole list, and then examine a couple of these
potential pitfalls in detail:

1. *Finances*: Leaders, particularly those who have power posi-
   tions and make important decisions concerning finances,
   tend to use practices that may encourage incorrect
   handling of finances and eventually wrong use. A character trait of greed often is rooted deep and eventually will
   cause impropriety with regard to finances.

2. *Power*: Leaders who are effective in ministry must use various power bases in order to accomplish their ministry. With power so available and being used almost daily, there is a tendency to abuse it.

3. *Pride*: Pride can lead to the downfall of a leader. As a leader there is a dynamic tension that must be maintained. We must have a healthy respect for ourselves, and yet we must recognize that we have nothing that was not given to us by God.

4. *Sex*: Illicit sexual relationships have been a major downfall both in the Bible and in Western cultures. Joseph's classic integrity check with respect to sexual sin is the ideal model that should be in leaders' minds.

5. *Family*: Problems between spouses or between parents and children or between siblings can destroy a leader's ministry. What is needed are biblical values lived out with regard to husband-wife relationships, parent-children relationships, and sibling relationships.

6. *Plateauing*: Leaders who are competent tend to plateau. Their very strength becomes a weakness. They can continue to minister at a level without there being a reality or Spirit-empowered renewing effect.[1]

In my years of coaching, I have seen each of these six downfalls rear its ugly head and ruin lives, but two seem to be more prevalent than any of the others: financial abuse and illicit sex. In order to keep your life and your family from being ravaged by the effects of these poisons, you must build thick hedges of protection around yourself.

## Financial Hedges

Financial mismanagement can wreak havoc in both your family and your church. Money problems are not only the number one reason for divorce in the United States, but also the reason that countless ministries close their doors every year. The way you choose to handle your finances is not just about you. Your decisions will greatly affect the health of your family and the future of your church. If you aren't careful, your personal stewardship habits can be the lid on what God wants to do in your life and in your ministry.

I learned this lesson firsthand when I moved to New York to start The Journey Church of the City. Working my way along the ministry track over the preceding few years, I had racked up some personal debt. Just after Kelley and I got to New York and began preparing for The Journey's launch, I felt God telling me that I should get rid of that debt—that it was going to hurt what God wanted to do through me and through The Journey. I had this unshakable sense that I couldn't lead a new church well if I was enslaved to creditors (see Prov. 22:7).

I wasn't excited by the insight. After all, I had just left a good position in California and moved to the most expensive city in the country. I had sacrificed all of my savings and most of my possessions for this privilege. Suddenly I was paying more in rent for a one-bedroom apartment than the mortgage on my house had been. I was working a full-time mainstream job, making less money than I'd ever made in my life, and trying to start a church to boot.

God didn't seem to care about my excuses; He was all over me about this issue. Apparently, He knew that if I didn't get my finances under control at that point, they would become a major problem later in my life. So, I gathered all of my bills together, added them up, and discovered that I was $16,000 in debt. The number shocked me. I had been living in denial about how much debt I had actually accumulated. I began to study what the Bible says about money, and then I put together a 36-month plan for getting my financial house in order. God blessed my humble efforts; Kelley and I were

out of debt within 18 months. (For the full audio teaching on my 36-month plan, go to www.RenegadePastorBook.com and download *Debt-Free Pastor*.)

As I shared my story with other pastor friends, I learned that I wasn't the only one who had gotten caught in the debt trap. Most pastors could use some help in this area. Could you? When was the last time you took a hard look at your family's financial health? I encourage you to get honest with yourself about the current state of your finances. You can never get to where you want to be unless you have an accurate understanding of your starting point. Ask God to guide you in getting this area of your life under control. The future of your family depends on it more than you may realize. Here are a few practical hedges you can begin building to make sure that mismanaged personal finances don't become a downfall for you:

- *Tithe faithfully.* You will never have financial peace if you aren't honoring God with the full tithe. According to God's math, you'll be able to live with much less stress on 90% of tithed income than you will on 100% of non-tithed income. Test Him in this area; He is faithful (see Mal. 3:10). For an in-depth study of biblical giving, see my book *The Generosity Ladder: Your Next Step to Financial Peace.*[2]

- *Create a financial margin.* No matter how stretched your money feels at the moment, you can make a decision to create a financial margin in your life. Financial pressure is rarely an income problem; it's almost always an outgo problem. Begin looking at ways you can restructure your expenses and eliminate any unnecessary spending. Most people live on roughly 110 percent of their income, which keeps them in constant bondage. If you can discipline yourself to live on 70 percent of your income, you will be able to set yourself up for a lifetime of financial peace and avoid the danger that comes with living beyond your means. (Visit www.RenegadePastorBook.com

for the "70 Percent Principle of Lasting Wealth" worksheet. It will help you discover where your money should be going.)

- *Get and stay out of debt.* The Bible is clear that no one should be in debt to another person (see Rom. 13:8), yet we live in a culture where debt is the norm. But, as my friend Dave Ramsey likes to point out, normal in America is broke. So who wants to be normal? One of the most important hedges you can build to protect your personal finances is to make the decision to get and remain debt-free (except for a home mortgage) for the rest of your life. If you need help with a plan for paying off your current debt and learning to live without new debt going forward, I recommend Dave Ramsey's *Complete Guide to Money.*[3]

As a pastor, building hedges to protect your own financial house is only half of the equation. In addition to getting your personal resources under control, you also need hedges in place to mandate responsibility when it comes to the church's finances. I've known pastors who carried the church checkbook in their back pocket—not a wise move. There has to be accountability built into the financial process. One pastor I knew lost his church and his family when someone figured out that he had stolen over half a million dollars from the church over a 10-year period. He had been siphoning the church's income into his own bank account bit by bit.

Now, I know you think you would never do such a thing—and you probably wouldn't. But you need to have regulations in place to remove even the possibility of temptation. Besides, thick hedges can keep you from the appearance of impropriety, protecting your reputation and ultimately your ministry if questions are ever raised about the handling of finances. At The Journey, I wouldn't know how to get my hands on money without others knowing even if I wanted to. We have guidelines set up for submitting a request for funds, and I have to play by the rules just like everyone else. I'm not going to outline specific practices you should put in place for your

church; those are up to you and your staff. But I do implore you to put some safe distance between yourself and any possibility of financial mismanagement or irresponsibility.

## Sexual Hedges

While sexual temptation is a hot topic for almost everyone, pastors are under particular attack in this area—and fall victim to the attack way too often. You don't have to look far to find example after example of major ministries that have been obliterated by sexual indiscretion. You are probably also aware of many less well-known examples of churches, reputations and families being devastated by marital infidelity. The devil loves to work through sexual temptation, and no one is immune—not even you.

The question isn't whether or not you will be tempted sexually; the question is how you can keep yourself at the safest distance possible from inevitable temptation—and then how you will deal with it when it does sneak in. The single best way to protect yourself, your marriage, your family and your ministry from the ravages of sexual misconduct is to build large, intentional hedges into your life.

Several years ago, Jerry Jenkins, the author of the best-selling *Left Behind* series, wrote a book on this issue called *Hedges: Loving Your Marriage Enough to Protect It.*[4] If you haven't read it, I encourage you to do so. In the book, Jenkins details some of the protective hedges he has put in place to proactively protect his marriage from the damage he knows the enemy wants to inflict on it. I have taken these hedges to heart and have been applying most of them to my life since my wedding day. They are not always easy or practical to adhere to—and have led to embarrassing situations from time to time—but I am willing to do whatever it takes to stay far away from any impropriety that has the potential to ruin my life. Are you? Here are a few hedges I would recommend putting in place:

> *Don't dine, travel or meet with a member*
> *of the opposite sex alone.*

Is there anything technically wrong with having a private meeting, sharing a meal or traveling with someone of the opposite sex? No. But is it a wise move if you are married? Absolutely not. Personally, I believe that spending time alone with a woman other than my wife, even if there's no questionable intent on either side, can open the door to all kinds of problems—not the least of which is my becoming comfortable being alone with a woman who is not my wife. As a leader, I want to stay above even the appearance of indiscretion. I also don't want to do anything that would make my wife uncomfortable. Here are some practical tips for building this hedge:

- If you need to meet with a member of the opposite sex in a non-windowed room, leave the door wide open or invite a third party to the meeting.

- Don't go to a restaurant alone with a member of the opposite sex, even if it's to discuss ministry concerns. Always take a third person with you.

- Don't allow a member of the opposite sex to pick you up at the airport. I can't tell you how many times I've heard male friends say they thought another man was picking them up from the airport, but something came up and the man's wife came instead. Don't put yourself in that situation. Your marriage and reputation are worth far more than the cost of a rental car.

- Be careful about staying in other people's homes. Early in my ministry, I preached a small-town revival. The pastor of the church holding the revival asked me to stay at his home. I was young and on a shoestring budget, so I agreed. The morning after I preached, I woke up and walked into the kitchen—where the pastor's wife was sitting alone, having a

cup of coffee. Her husband had been called into a meeting at the church, so it was just the two of us. Needless to say, I got out of there as fast as I could. Now I prefer hotels, but if staying in someone's home is unavoidable, I bring another pastor or a friend with me.

*If you are going to hug someone of the opposite sex, only do so in front of others.*

For men, and perhaps for women too, there's the potential to enjoy hugging a member of the opposite sex a little too much. That burst of sexual energy you may get from pressing against another person in a full frontal hug can lead to a domino effect of thoughts and feelings. If you think this could be an issue for you, hugging a member of the opposite sex just isn't worth the risk. If you want to make physical contact, stick to a side hug.

On a related note, if you do experience a burst of attraction for someone other than your spouse, you need to deal with it right away. When you hug someone and feel a little too much, when someone in the congregation makes your heart start beating faster, or when you catch someone's eye and feel a rush of desire, do you have a trusted person you can turn to who can act as a lightning rod for you? Someone who can help you ground that electricity as soon as it hits? Let me explain:

A lightning rod is a conductor positioned to receive any bolt of electricity that threatens a house. The rod absorbs the electrical current (lightning) when it hits and pulls it away from the house, through a wire that runs into the ground. Thanks to the lightning rod, potential disaster is avoided. To avert the disaster that is possible when lightning strikes you in the form of sexual temptation, you need a lightning rod in place to absorb and redirect the current. Otherwise, you may end up electrocuted.

A friend of mine, Wayne Cordeiro, first introduced me to this concept during a leadership summit at Willow Creek Community

Church in Illinois. Wayne explained that everyone needs a lightning rod—a mature friend or mentor with whom you can share difficult situations; someone who can absorb the shock of the problems and/or temptations that hit you and help minimize the ripple effect by running interference, giving sound advice, and pushing you to maintain the right perspective.

I happen to be on staff with several other pastors whom I would trust with my life. I've learned to go to them immediately if someone catches my attention and say, "She caught my eye. I don't know why. Don't let me talk to her." Usually, the process of making one of my lightning rods aware of the electricity is all it takes to calm the adrenaline. I may see the same woman again the next week—even get a side hug—and have no reaction, because the current has been grounded. The devil wants to keep the thoughts and feelings that follow those bursts of sexual energy in the dark, because bringing them into the light destroys them. If you don't have a lightning rod in your life, I encourage you to begin cultivating one.

*Avoid any kind of flirtation with someone*
*other than your spouse.*

Idle flirting seems harmless on the surface, but it's deceivingly dangerous. It is a step down a path you don't want to be on. Men and women are both highly susceptible to flattery and can latch on all too quickly to anyone who gives them the attention they crave. You never know what may be going on in the life of the person with whom you are innocently flirting that could cause her to think it means something more. Illustrating the power of what you may consider to be "harmless" words, James writes, "A tiny spark can set a great forest on fire" (Jas. 3:5).

Avoid any kind of conversation or interaction with members of the opposite sex that could be considered flirting. That energy and attention should be reserved for your spouse. Here are some practical steps you can take to build and stay behind this hedge:

- Never compliment someone of the opposite sex on his or her looks; if you must offer some sort of affirmation, stick to complimenting clothing.

- Wear your wedding ring. If you are talking with a member of the opposite sex, make sure it is visible.

- Flirt with your spouse heavily and often. Surprise her with a wink from across the room or a game of footsie under the dinner table.

- As early as possible when talking to someone new, let that person know you are a Christian.

As you begin planting hedges in your life, remember to plant them higher, wider and thicker than you think you need to. Some of what I've outlined here may seem extreme to you; that's because hedges should be built with plenty of margin in mind. Don't build them just big enough to do the trick. Build them so high, so thick and so wide that you would have a hard time getting around or through them if you tried.

## Hard Work

Providing well for your family is a major component of loving them—and hard work is key to being able to provide well. For some reason, however, too many pastors have gotten it into their heads that ministry is a soft profession—that it can be done with less effort and intentionality than other jobs. In a surprising number of ministerial circles, laziness has become commonplace. What a gross disservice to the calling placed on a pastor's life! As a pastor, you have been called to minister to God's people with an excellence that reflects His own. You have a higher, more intense responsibility to work hard and do your work well than just about anyone else.

Historically, the three classic professions in Western civilization have been doctors, lawyers and ministers. That's right—doctors and lawyers are your peer group. As such, I would argue that they should be your point of comparison when it comes to hard work. Compared to the hours the average doctor or lawyer puts in, you have a pretty good life, right? You don't have to run to the emergency room for an 8-hour surgery at 3:00 in the morning or spend 13 hours a day poring over briefs. But you should expect to expend the same level of energy and commitment in your work as these other two professions do. Allowing your family to see you working diligently in order to provide for them, to accomplish things in ministry, and to be a good leader is a gift you give them on a daily basis.

A few years ago, I was at a local conference with a pastor friend. From the stage, one of the speakers built the case that, as a pastor, you should be home when your kids arrive from school every afternoon. He laid it on really thick, hitting every emotional nerve possible. After the lunch break that day, I couldn't find my friend. When I called to see where he was, he told me he had run home to meet the school bus. There was just one problem—his kids weren't on the bus. Apparently they had afterschool activities, so he was sitting around an empty house wasting time. Thanks to the guilt the speaker had associated with work, my friend missed the next session of the conference and some great growth opportunities—for nothing.

Don't allow anyone to make you feel guilty for being a hard worker; you are called to work hard. In fact, according to the Bible, if you can work and you don't, you shouldn't eat (see 2 Thess. 3:10). By choosing to be committed to work, you may miss some Little League games, but that's okay. You don't have to be at every one. There's a balance to be struck. As long as your family is in its rightful position in your life, you will actually be setting a strong example for your kids when you do have to miss their activities from time to time. You will be showing them that you are working hard for them and for the Kingdom. You will be earning their respect and teaching them a work ethic that will serve them well down the road.

As you commit to actively loving your family by marking out boundaries to strengthen your relationships, by building hedges to protect them, and by applying yourself to hard work, you will be taking a major step toward renegade living. Average pastors, even well-intentioned ones, allow their relationships with their spouse and kids to barrel ahead with no boundaries or hedges in place. Average pastors buy into the myth that hard work isn't necessary in ministry—and they suffer the consequences. Renegade pastors do the opposite. In doing so, they reflect the excellence of God to a watching world, enjoy a healthy family life, and leave a legacy of love for generations to come.

## Renegade Pastor Testimony

I'm embarrassed to say that for many years my family paid the price for my being in ministry. They always got my leftovers—my leftover time, energy and attention. I knew they deserved more, but I wasn't sure how to give it. I've learned (and am still learning) that prioritizing my family not only makes my family happier, but it also makes my ministry more fulfilling.

As a pastor, I have always felt overwhelmed with stuff to do. I would even brag about my workaholic tendencies and how long it had been since my last day off—until Nelson set me straight. He suggested starting a "What Not to Do" list of things I was doing that I shouldn't be doing. Now, not only do I do more in less time, but I'm also doing the *right* things! Life-giving.

Jamey Stuart, Senior Pastor
Believers Church—Chesapeake, Virginia

# *Commitment Three:*
# Fulfill Your Calling

*Becoming All God Has Called You to Be*

To avoid criticism, say nothing, do nothing, be nothing.
ARISTOTLE

I pray . . . that you will keep on growing in knowledge
and understanding. For I want you to understand
what really matters, so that you may live pure and
blameless lives until the day of Christ's return.
PAUL (PHILIPPIANS 1:9-10)

Imagine you are sitting in your office one afternoon when the phone rings. You pick it up, and on the other end of the line, you hear the voice of an influential figure you greatly respect. Pick whomever you like—Billy Graham, the President, a famous sports figure— it doesn't matter; this is your visualization. You're so shocked this person is calling you that it takes you a minute to steady yourself. Your mind is racing, trying to figure out what in the world is going on. After a few minutes of chitchat (about ministering to world leaders? the state of the Union? winning championships?) this person you revere shocks you all over again by inviting you to come speak to a group of people he's pulling together. He says he has heard good things about you and he thinks you would be the

perfect keynote speaker for his event. He gives you a topic—something you've never spoken on before—and hangs up.

You lean back in your chair, trying to convince yourself that the phone call really happened. Once you're sure you weren't dreaming, a sense of urgency sets in. You shift into high gear to get ready for the talk. You start gathering information on the assigned topic, reading everything you can get your hands on, talking to people, looking up quotes and studying, all the while praying for God's guidance and wisdom. You thank God that you have a few weeks to get ready for the big moment, because you need time to pull everything together and let it marinate. Obviously, when the phone rang, you weren't already equipped with what you would need to meet the challenge. You will have to gather, organize and internalize the elements that will prepare you to succeed at what you've been called on to do. You will have to go through a process of working, learning, practicing, studying and growing as much as you can between now and your moment of truth.

 ## Renegade Commitment Three: Fulfill Your Calling

While this scenario may sound farfetched, it's not all that different from your call to ministry. When God first let you know He wanted you to be a messenger for His kingdom, you didn't have everything required to be successful. You likely didn't have much of anything. I know I didn't. Humbled by the call, you started a long process of gathering the tools you would need to fulfill it. You began to cultivate insights, biblical knowledge, like-minded friends, wise counselors, communication and leadership skills, maturity, accountability, a team . . . the list goes on. If you are still growing in your life and ministry, you have undoubtedly discovered that this gathering process never ends. Whether you have been at this for 2 years or 20 years, you have to do your part every single day to fulfill the calling God has placed on you. As you do, you honor the third commitment of being a renegade pastor.

## Tender and Tough

Early in my own ministry, I met a man named Ralph Carpenter. Ralph pastored some large churches in the Southeast from the 1960s through the 1990s. By the time I connected with him, he was an old man eager to pour into the next generation. Ralph and I developed a close relationship, and he took to mentoring me. He helped me begin the process of gathering the things I would need to fulfill my calling. We started having breakfast together about once a month at his house. We would sit around his old wooden table, and he would tell me everything he knew about pastoring in a God-honoring way.

One morning as we were sitting over coffee, our meal long finished, Ralph said to me, "Nelson, you need two things to survive in ministry: a tender heart and a tough hide." As Ralph went on to explain, having a heart that's sensitive toward lost people and toward the ravages of sin in the world is crucial to being able to minister well. But just as crucial, he emphasized, is having a thick skin toward the inevitable critics and attacks of the devil that accompany any effective ministry work. Trouble comes when these two things get inverted, as often happens with average pastors. While tough hearts and tender hides are all too common, they are the ingredients of a ministry that misses the mark of God's calling.

### Renegade Pastor Testimony

I know God has called me to be a pastor of His people. I know this because I can't do anything else in life and be fulfilled. I've tried! However, ministry is sometimes a difficult and frustrating calling. In the past, when I was struggling, I would become depressed and simply go through the motions until I would want to move to another work or maybe just give up. Nelson, however, drives home in his coaching the importance of remembering your call; because of this, remembering my call is now a major component of my life.

> My sense of calling gives me a constant renewal of purpose, a constant renewal of hope, and a constant renewal of vision. It gives me courage to know that the devil and all the traps, troubles, turmoil and tension he may throw my way are nothing compared to my calling from the mighty One, Jesus the living Christ!
>
> Kevin Hill, Senior Pastor
> Holley Church—Sweet Home, Oregon

## A Tender Heart

Keeping a tender heart isn't something that happens by default; it takes intentional nurturing. When I was living in New York City full-time, one of my favorite things to do was to go sit at an outdoor café in my neighborhood and watch the people stream by. In a 30-minute span, I would see hundreds of people going about their daily lives—couples with kids in tow, business people rushing to meetings, senior citizens out for a stroll, and teenagers laughing their way down the sidewalks. As the parade unfolded in front of me, I would remind myself that at least 80 percent of the people walking by were unchurched. Statistically speaking, I was likely the only Christian at the café—maybe the only Christian on the block. That realization stoked a huge sense of responsibility within me.

These days I make my home in South Florida rather than New York City, but I still spend time studying the people in my community—especially if I'm frustrated or discouraged over something that's going on at the church. Just the other day, I sat in my car outside a busy local restaurant and watched people come and go. I examined their faces, trying to see the struggles behind the smiles and wondering what kind of pain was causing the frowns. I prayed that God would help me see them as He does, and that He would keep my heart soft toward their problems and needs.

Spending time focusing on the people in the community where I minister grounds me. It reminds me why I do what I do, even when things are hard. I encourage you to give this exercise a try. Next time

you have the chance, spend a few minutes people watching. Take a fresh look at your neighbors and ask God to give you a soft heart toward them. Intentionally shifting your perspective off of your agenda and toward the people God has put around you—the people He is calling you to reach—goes a long way toward keeping your heart tender.

## A Tough Hide

If you are going to fulfill your calling, not only does your heart need to be tender, but your hide also needs to be tough. As you pursue God's purposes, you are going to face negativity and criticism. I guarantee it. Complacent Christians will rise up against you, and the devil will come after you. You can please some of the people all of the time and all of the people some of the time, but you will never please all of the people all of the time. The only way to avoid being questioned and criticized is to stop doing the things God is calling you to do—and you know as well as I do that that's not an option. Criticism is an unavoidable part of ministry, so you have to learn to handle it in a healthy way.

 You can please some of the people all of the time and all of the people some of the time, but you will never please all of the people all of the time.

Allowing critics to shape your path or discourage you does not honor God. Letting their pessimism rent space in your head can cause you to make decisions outside of God's will, which can lead to missing your calling altogether. Jesus faced criticism; Paul faced criticism; the disciples faced criticism; I face criticism; you face criticism. Given this reality, developing a tough hide—that is, learning how to deal with criticism well—is key to fulfilling your purpose. Here are four tips to help you stay strong when negativity tries to chafe you:

## 1. Strengthen Your Foundation

When your foundation is solid, criticism blows by you like a passing storm. It may cause you to bend a little from time to time, but it will never be able to move or break you. The best way to strengthen your foundation is to go deeper in your relationship with God through continual prayer and study of the Word. As you draw close to God, He will draw close to you (see Jas. 4:8). When that happens—when you are in constant, deep communion with your Father—you are better able to hear from Him in every decision you make, which will naturally diminish the voices of the critics when they come against you. If you know you are in the center of God's will, other opinions lose their strength.

When I first started realizing the importance of having a tough hide in the face of criticism, I remember thinking to myself, *Man, I'm not going to be a very good leader, because people's opinions matter way too much to me.* I am a people pleaser by nature. With growth, I came to realize that my number one concern needed to be to please God, not people. If I simply focused on pleasing Him, everything else would fall into place. I love these words from Paul:

> As for me, it matters very little how I might be evaluated by you or by any human authority. I don't even trust my own judgment on this point. My conscience is clear, but that doesn't prove I'm right. It is the Lord himself who will examine me and decide (1 Cor. 4:3-4).

Allow criticism to draw you closer to God. As you strengthen your foundation, critics' words may still try to wound you, but they won't be able to.

## 2. Limit Your Exposure

Minimize the criticism that comes across your desk. You are not a trashcan. There will always be negativity trying to creep in by way of anonymous emails, unsigned letters, or miffed people who want

to march right into your office and tell you what they think. If you are serious about protecting your ministry—not to mention your personal well-being—begin building some criticism hedges around yourself. One great way to limit your exposure is to set up a gatekeeper who takes a first look at all of your email and standard mail before it ever makes it to you. I recommend asking a trusted staff member to take on the responsibility. This gatekeeper will become invaluable to you.

Smaller-level gatekeepers can be helpful as well. For example, at The Journey, we use Connection Cards to communicate with everyone in our services. Each week, all of our guests, regular attenders and members fill out a Connection Card and drop it in the offering bucket. (For more on using Connection Cards, see my book *Fusion: Turning First-Time Guests into Fully Engaged Members of Your Church*,[1] and visit www.RenegadePastorBook. com.) On the back of the card, there is a designated space for questions, comments and prayer requests. About once a month, someone will use the space to spew negativity—writing something like, "You aren't deep enough" or "You're ugly and your mama dresses you funny." Every staff member who handles Connection Cards knows to weed these comments out before I see them. I don't need to be aware of unproductive, spiteful negativity—and neither do you.

Guard your focus, your motivation and your energy. Protect yourself and keep the negativity at arm's length. You are, after all, responsible for leading God's church. It's only wise to limit your exposure to the arrows that are trying to pierce the heart of your mission. I am in no way implying that you should ignore all criticism. I am not suggesting that you run away and pretend it doesn't exist. Simply guard your heart with wisdom, and allow others to help you choose what's worth addressing and what isn't. Still, no matter how well you limit your exposure, there will inevitably be times when you have to face the music, which leads me to . . .

## 3. Master the Art of Confrontation

Situations will arise that call for confrontation. When they do, you have to have the courage to sit down with the person or group bringing the criticism and address the issue head on. Over the years—both at The Journey and in working with other church leaders—I have found that when the pastor goes directly to a critic to address his or her grievances, the result is positive about 70 percent of the time. Don't be afraid to confront conflict when necessary. Just keep these four things in mind:

- *Pray and Prep*: Before you sit down with anyone eyeball to eyeball, take the time to pray over the situation in general and over the meeting you are about to have specifically. Pray that you won't be driven by your emotions, but that you will stay grounded. Also, make some notes about what you want to say in the meeting. They will serve as a guideline to keep things on track. In short, be prepared.

- *Plan Your Approach*: When you step into a conflict-resolution situation, your approach will influence the outcome. So, think about your approach before you meet with your critic. Typically, I recommend taking the angle of resolution through clarification. Start by shouldering some responsibility with a statement like, "I just want to clarify . . ." or "Maybe we didn't thoroughly explain _____ and that has led to some concern . . ." This approach usually disarms the critic, keeps you from being in defense-mode (which is key), and often leads to the solution. Sometimes the critic really is unclear on an issue, and that lack of clarity is what has led to the criticism. As you think about your approach, above all else make sure that you are entering into the conversation with the goal of preserving your relationship with the other person. You can be direct while still reflecting the love of God.

- *Assess the Attitude (Never Assume)*: Along the same lines, make sure you confront the attitude, confusion or motive that's driving the attack, rather than confronting the person. In your process of assessing that attitude, never assume anything. If you aren't sure what has led to the issue, ask. After all, you know what happens when you assume, right?

- *Act Early*: It's natural to want to shrink from confrontation. I know I have been guilty of turning a blind eye to a situation that needs addressing, hoping everything will work out on its own. After this mindset had gotten me into trouble more than once, a mentor of mine taught me an invaluable lesson: Run to conflict. If you catch conflict in its earliest stages—before it becomes infectious, takes on armor, and runs people out of the church—you can arrest it and correct it. Avoidance produces misery. Run to conflict in the same way David ran to Goliath when everyone else ran in the opposite direction.

Recently, I faced a situation at The Journey that required me to call on these tenets of confrontation. An individual who had just married one of the Team Leaders in our church wrote a scathing comment on the back of the Connection Card. The comment was in reference to a change we had made in our worship services. This criticism made it to me for two reasons: (1) the critic was the spouse of someone in a leadership position, and (2) the criticism was regarding the service rather than something of a personal nature. At first I thought, *Well, everybody adjusts to change in different ways,* and decided to let it go. Two weeks later, this person reiterated the same criticism on the back of the Connection Card. I knew I had to act.

After service the next Sunday, I pulled the person aside and said, "I see that you've written this twice now, so I just wanted to talk with you to see if I can be of any help. I don't want to read into the emotion behind your comments, so why don't you tell me exactly what your concern is?" Once the person expressed the concern to me

verbally, I knew this was nothing more than an issue of clarification. I explained why we had made the change to the service and how the change was a good move for our services overall.

The response? "Oh, I never thought of it like that. That actually makes sense." Bingo.

Having to pull this person aside after a service wasn't easy. It required having a tough hide. The situation was uncomfortable for a couple of minutes, but a simple clarification solved everything. Now my relationship with that person is stronger than it was before. The pain of the confrontation was worth it for the sake of the positive outcome. Had I not confronted the situation head-on, things could have turned out very differently. When people are slightly off course, give them the benefit of the doubt and handle them with care.

Unfortunately, things don't always work out so well. Thirty percent of the time, there will be real friction. Messes happen. When you confront a situation that may not resolve smoothly, make sure you have thought through possible solutions. You may need to stop someone's ascent up the leadership ranks in your church. You may need to ask someone to leave the congregation. Confrontation isn't easy. Let the fact that you will get favorable resolutions 70 percent of the time bolster your confidence as you run toward conflict and face your critics with grace.

## 4. Find a Lightning Rod

As I mentioned in the last chapter, finding a lightning rod to help ground the negative energy that comes your way is critical to your ministry—and not just when it comes to improper sexual energy. You also need a lightning rod to help you deal with criticism. My friend Wayne (the one who introduced me to this concept) once told me that for many years he made the common mistake of using his wife as a lightning rod in this area. When he faced criticism at church, he would go home and tell his wife, "You won't believe what so-and-so said to me." As you can imagine, it was all too easy for his wife to begin harboring feelings of resentment towards that person. She's human.

But then, when Wayne and the criticizer reconciled, he would often forget to tell his wife that things had been resolved. So even though the situation may have found a positive end, Wayne's wife could easily still have a tainted view of the congregant—and that's not good.

So, don't make your spouse your lightning rod. Find a more objective candidate. The ideal person for this position would be a friend—maybe even a pastor—from another church. Sometimes lightning rods come in groups. Maybe you have a group of guys who would qualify. You need to make sure these are people with whom you can share the onslaught of criticisms you are facing and who are spiritually mature enough to give their opinions in a helpful, non-biased way. If you absorb all of the shock of criticism yourself, you will constantly feel like you are on fire. Your ministry and your life will reflect the stress you are experiencing. Even a tough hide doesn't qualify you to go it on your own. (For a more in-depth discussion on managing criticism, download my free *How to Handle Criticism* e-book at www.RenegadePastorBook.com. You may even want to study the e-book together with your staff.)

My wise pastor friend Ralph told me something else, as we sat around that old breakfast table, that I've never forgotten: "If you go too long without meeting the devil head-on, it could be because you're traveling in the same direction." A little bit of spiritual warfare is a sign you are making progress. Things are going to go wrong. The devil is going to throw up roadblocks. People are going to criticize you. If you want to fulfill your calling, you are going to have to face that spiritual warfare along the way. As you move through it, keep your heart tender and your hide tough—and never stop gathering. Never stop preparing for the task you've been called to do.

### Renegade Pastor Testimony

After 35 years in ministry, I found myself wanting to serve God more than ever, but I was handling all areas of the church's work. I didn't realize how important it was to allow

others to help with the ministry. Nelson made a statement that resonated with me: He said, "Your church won't grow if you aren't growing." So I began to set a course in my life and ministry to grow myself and invest in others what God has been pouring into my life. I am indebted to Nelson for coming alongside me at a time when I was dry and felt washed up. Now I have new drive to serve God like never before.

Harold Phillips, Pastor
River Oaks Christian Church—Jenks, Oklahoma

## The Call to Prepare

The call to ministry is the call to prepare—and preparation is an ongoing process. You will never learn all there is to be learned about any subject; you'll never reach the pinnacle point in any area. And who would want to? It's the continual reaching that grows you, equipping you to live and minster at an ever-increasing level. Part of being an effective pastor and a more fulfilled person is deciding to be a lifelong learner.

One common mistake pastors make is to focus too much attention on growing their churches, while failing to prepare themselves personally for leading at a higher level. Personal growth always precedes healthy church growth. If the church's growth begins to outpace the pastor's personal growth, cracks become evident pretty quickly. Given this reality, creating a personal growth plan is key to fulfilling your calling. Take a look at these six primary ways God grows you:

1. God grows you as you study *Scripture*.
2. God grows you as you seek Him in *prayer*.
3. God grows you through the internal witness of the *Holy Spirit*.
4. God grows you through the *books* you read.
5. God grows you through the *people* you meet.
6. God grows you through the *circumstances* you face.

You can't always control the circumstances you face. You can't control what God wants to do in you through the Holy Spirit. But you can control how you cooperate with Him by reading His Word, spending time with Him in prayer, and seeking out knowledge through books and other resources. You can put yourself around other passionate leaders who are committed to God's purposes. In short, you can develop a growth plan that will continually move you toward being the person you need to be to fulfill your calling.

A good personal growth plan is anchored by four cornerstones: the books you read, the audio teaching you listen to, the seminars and conferences you attend, and the coaching to which you submit yourself.

## Books

As English playwright Joseph Addison once said, "Reading is to the mind what exercise is to the body." Without reading, your growth atrophies. Books have the ability to expand you and your ministry in unique ways. Whether you currently consider yourself an avid reader or not, you can develop this all-important skill. I will confess that for the first 17 years of my life, I probably didn't read a single book from start to finish. Cliff Notes got me through school. When I went into ministry, though, I knew that my becoming a reader was critical for both my own growth and my church's health. Understanding the truth behind the old adage that leaders are readers, I prayed for God to make me into a reader. I am happy to say that He answered my prayer. I now read about five books every week.

 Creating a personal growth plan is key to fulfilling your calling.

While there's a place for reading novels and other leisure material, the reading habit I encourage you to develop as part of your personal growth plan focuses on books that can serve as a catalyst to fulfilling your calling. Developing a system will help you become a

more effective reader and keep you focused on material that matters. I suggest balancing your reading around five types of books:

## 1. The Bible

The centerpiece of your reading plan should be the Bible. Some years you will want to read straight through from Genesis to Revelation, while other years you will go more slowly, concentrating on certain books and passages. The Scripture itself doesn't change, but the application to your life can change with every reading (see Heb. 4:12). Spend personal time in the Bible every day. Let it saturate your being.

## 2. Best Practice Books

Next, focus on best practice books. Best practice books are tools to help you develop personally and grow your church. This book could be considered a best practice book, as could any of my books on creating healthy church systems. (See www.RenegadePastorBook. com for an expanded bibliography of each of my books.) Business books like Jim Collins's *Good to Great* or Peter Drucker's *The Effective Executive* also fall into the best practices category. Focus on books you can read relatively quickly and that have good application points for where you are. (For an in-depth list of best practice recommendations, go to www.RenegadePastorBook.com.) In addition to your regular Bible reading, I suggest reading one best practice book every month and then working the next three types of books around the edges of your reading plan.

## 3. History Books—Biography and Church History

A wise person once said, "Those who don't understand the mistakes of the past are doomed to repeat them." To be an effective leader, you need to have a grasp on history—especially the history of the church. After all, you are part of that history in the making. Start learning all you can about early church history and work your way through modern times. In addition, I suggest picking up biographies of great historical leaders, from both within and outside the church.

You can glean a lot of insight from their stories of struggle and triumph. Obviously, these are books you will read a little more slowly. To get started, try putting one history book on your reading list every year. (For a suggested reading list of church history books and biographies, go to www.RenegadePastorBook.com.)

## 4. Theology Books

You may have done a lot of theological reading in seminary, but don't let that be an excuse not to take your study to the next level. Now that you are a practitioner, you have a different mindset than you did in seminary. Choose to spend time becoming ever more familiar with Christian theology, systematic theology, concise theology, and the like. To keep growing as a pastor, you need to be going continually deeper in your theological understanding. (For a suggested theological reading list, go to www.RenegadePastorBook.com.)

## 5. Philosophy Books—Christian and Western

A basic understanding of both Christian and Western philosophy can be extremely beneficial. Books about the Western intellectual tradition will give you insight into how our society came to operate by its current mindset. Exploring the driving forces of culture can go a long way toward helping you influence it. (For a suggested philosophical reading list, go to www.RenegadePastorBook.com.)

To balance your reading between these five areas, try sticking to a reading plan like this:

| The Renegade Reading Plan | | | |
|---|---|---|---|
| **January** | Bible | Best Practice Book 1 | Theology Book 1 (read first third) |
| **February** | Bible | Best Practice Book 2 | Theology Book 1 (read second third) |
| **March** | Bible | Best Practice Book 3 | Theology Book 1 (read third third) |

| The Renegade Reading Plan (con't) | | | |
|---|---|---|---|
| **April** | Bible | Best Practice Book 4 | History Book 1 (read first third) |
| **May** | Bible | Best Practice Book 5 | History Book 1 (read second third) |
| **June** | Bible | Best Practice Book 6 | History Book 1 (read third third) |
| **July** | Bible | Best Practice Book 7 | Philosophy Book 1 (read first third) |
| **August** | Bible | Best Practice Book 8 | Philosophy Book 1 (read second third) |
| **September** | Bible | Best Practice Book 9 | Philosophy Book 1 (read third third) |
| **October** | Bible | Best Practice Book 10 | Theology Book 2 (read first third) |
| **November** | Bible | Best Practice Book 11 | Theology Book 2 (read second third) |
| **December** | Bible | Best Practice Book 12 | Theology Book 2 (read third third) |
| **January** | Bible | Best Practice Book 13 | History Book 2 (read first third). . . and so forth . . . |

One more suggestion as you develop your personal reading plan: Never waste time reading a bad book. Your time is too precious and there are too many good books out there. If you get partway through a book and it's just not speaking to you, you don't have to finish it. It's okay to trash it and move on to something better. (For my very practical "How to Read More" resource, go to www. RenegadePastorBook.com.)

## Audio Resources

When your hands are busy but your mind is free, audio resources are a great way to keep learning and growing. From audio books to packaged teaching by leaders you respect to various nuts and bolts podcasts, your iPod can become an effective educational tool.

Keep pouring the good stuff in. (For a list of recommended audio resources, go to www.RenegadePastorBook.com.)

## Seminars and Conferences

If you've been a pastor for very long, you know there's no shortage of conferences vying for your attendance. Be selective in deciding which ones you want to take advantage of. Several of the big, flashy conferences that get a lot of attention tend to give you more inspiration than practical application. I actually stopped going to a few of those because I wasn't walking away with enough action steps. After a couple of days, the high of the weekend would be gone, and nothing in my ministry would be changing. Be a wise steward of your time and money. Focus on conferences and seminars that help both you and your church advance toward the purposes God has for you. (For more information on the seminars I offer throughout the year, visit www.RenegadePastorBook.com.)

## Personal Coaching

Fulfilling your calling inherently means rising to the highest level of potential God has put in you. In order to reach your potential, you need a coach. Why shouldn't you? The greatest business leaders, entertainers and athletes the world has ever known have had coaches to guide them to the top of their game. Bill Gates has written about the power of coaching. Meryl Streep still works with an acting coach. Michael Jordan had a personal coach every year he played basketball. Even at the pinnacle of success, he knew he still needed someone training him, helping him and directing him to even higher levels of the potential within him. So do you.

As part of your personal growth plan, I strongly encourage you to submit yourself to coaching. Nothing can better equip you for the mission you've been called to. But be thoughtful in your choice. While there are a lot of people out there offering coaching for church leaders, not all coaches can give you applicable tools to meet you where your church is today and help you move it toward the future

God has in store. Be careful of coaches who don't have a proven track record of success. Also be wary of those who are not practitioners themselves, or who have been out of the ministry for a while. When it comes to coaching, relevance is paramount. Knowing what worked last week, last month or last year isn't nearly as important as knowing what's going to work next week, next month and next year.

My life's great passion is coaching leaders like you who are committed to partnering with God to unleash the full redemptive potential of their churches. If you'd like to find out more about the coaching I offer, visit www.RenegadePastorBook.com. I would be honored to work with you.

## Slack Leads to Lack

Think back for a moment to the differences between Alex Average and Rob Renegade. The majority of the issues Alex struggles with in his life and ministry can be traced to a lack of intentionality. His heart is in the right place and his theology is sound; he simply hasn't made the decision to pick up and use the tools that can move him beyond average. He doesn't have what he needs to fulfill his calling and, for some reason, he has stopped gathering. The slack in Alex's preparation has led to lack in his life and in his church.

Rob, on the other hand, hasn't lost sight of the task he was called to on the day God tapped him for ministry. He stays in preparation mode, constantly gathering what he needs to be able to fulfill his calling with excellence. Rob reads voraciously, listens to all of the audio teaching he can get his hands on, attends quality seminars and conferences, and engages in personal coaching. He intentionally fosters a tender heart and keeps his hide tough against criticism and attacks of the enemy. God is honoring Rob's efforts by developing him personally and growing a healthy church for him to lead.

If you want to be a renegade, you have to commit to fulfilling your calling. You have to commit to doing the work that it takes to grow—to resisting the slack that will try to creep into your life. Let

your prayer be for God to continually make you into the person you need to be to fulfill your calling today, next week, next month, next year and 10 years from now. Then put feet to that prayer by gathering what you need to meet the challenge and by developing a plan to take responsibility for your growth. When you do, you can rest in the assurance that you are partnering with God at the level He has called you to. You can rest in the assurance that one day, you will hear Him say, "Well done, my good and faithful servant" (Matt. 25:23).

## Renegade Pastor Testimony

For years I have talked with our church staff about the "invisible weight" that comes with leadership. This weight is both real and constant in any area of leadership (as a parent, a coach, a manager, etc.). The weight often can feel heavier in the environment of ministry. For a season, I was allowing the invisible weight of pastoring a church to be too much for me. Then Nelson gave me a principle of wisdom that changed everything. He defined what it looked like to work *on* the church versus working *in* the church. I was working *in* the church; and wherever the church went, I went—for good or for bad. It was an unhealthy and unsustainable approach to leading and greatly limited how I was overseeing the care and direction of our church. Once I removed myself from this limited perspective and moved to working *on* the church, things began to align. Now the invisible weight does not just rest on me individually, but is shared among our staff, group leaders, volunteer leaders and management teams. As a result, our church is so much healthier and better led than ever before. People are being cared for, needs are being met, ministry is taking place, and partners are being mobilized into ministry.

Joel Eason, Senior Pastor
Bridgeway Church—Tampa, Florida

# Commitment Four:
# Manage Your Time

*Taking Control of Your Most Limited Commodity*

Everything requires time. It is the only truly universal condition.
All work takes place in time and uses up time. Yet most people
take for granted this unique, irreplaceable, and necessary resource.
Nothing else, perhaps, distinguishes effective [people] as
much as their tender loving care of time.

PETER DRUCKER

Teach us to number our days, that we may gain a heart of wisdom.

KING DAVID (PSALM 90:12, *NIV*)

Remember the unexpected phone call you got from that person you admire? Well, he's calling again. This time it's early on a Monday morning. You're sitting in your office, looking over the schedule for the week ahead. It's shaping up to be an average to slightly heavy week. You're just filling in some details when the phone interrupts your train of thought. Picking it up, you hear your new friend's voice on the other end. He tells you how happy he is with the talk you gave at his event and offers you an unbelievable thank-you gift. His private jet is available for the weekend. If you can be ready to leave by Thursday at five o'clock, he will foot the bill for a relaxing getaway anywhere you want to go. He even promises to have you home in time to preach on Sunday.

What would his proposition do to your week? You would dive into your to-do list with fresh focus and diligence, wouldn't you? You would suddenly become more efficient, determined to get the week's work done by Thursday at five. After all, there's no way you could pass up the opportunity he's offering you—and you wouldn't have to. By simply managing your time more thoughtfully, you could do the same amount of work, with the same level of quality, and still be able to jump on that plane Thursday evening.

There's a principle at play here that I like to call the Week-Before-Vacation Principle. Most people get more done during the week before they take a vacation than at any other time during the year. Why? Because of one of the most basic truths of time management: Work expands to fill the time that's been allotted for it. Accordingly, when you know your time is limited, you manage it better. You prioritize differently. You work more efficiently. But why should that level of productivity only kick in the week before vacation? By adopting a few revolutionary time management concepts into your life, you can free up more hours in the day and more days in the month, in essence harnessing the Week-Before-Vacation Principle every week of the year.

 Work expands to fill the time that's been allotted for it.

As your time goes, so goes your life. Unless you steward your time wisely, there's no way to fulfill the purposes God has for you. You can't create more of this limited commodity, but you can learn to utilize what you have been given in a way that propels you to a higher level of living. As H. Jackson Brown Jr. writes, "You have exactly the same number of hours per day that were given to Helen Keller, Louis Pasteur, Michelangelo, Mother Teresa, Leonardo da Vinci, Thomas Jefferson, and Albert Einstein."[1] To put it in pastor terms, you have the same 24 hours a day given to John Wesley, Charles Spurgeon, C. S. Lewis, Billy Graham and every other notable, respected Christian

leader in the world. How you choose to view and use those 24 hours can transform you from a time-crunched average pastor to an effective renegade.

 **Renegade Commitment Four:** Manage Your Time

Average pastors take a passive approach to time. They let urgent matters and other people's agendas eat away hours rather than directing the current themselves. Renegade pastors, on the other hand, choose to honor God by intentionally making the most of every hour and every day. What type of time manager are you? Do you constantly feel like you are chasing the clock, or are you proactive in managing the most important resource you've been given? The greatest ministries require the greatest time management. The greatest lives do too. Here's the good news: You get to decide how well you do in this area. If you are ready to join the ranks of the renegades, it's time to embrace the fourth commitment of being a renegade pastor and learn to manage your time well. Here are 10 practices to help you get started right away:

## 1. Understand the Difference Between Efficient and Effective

You can be efficient without being effective, but it's hard to be effective without being efficient. Let me explain. Your efficiency hinges on how quickly you are able to do your work well. It's about being able to take a project that would take most people an hour to do and doing it in 50 minutes with the same level of excellence. Becoming more efficient is definitely a key to managing your time productively. But here's the catch: You can easily become efficient at doing things that don't matter.

While efficiency is about doing things well, effectiveness is about doing the right things well. The greatest time management question you can ask yourself is: Does this need to be done at all? Spending your limited time on something you don't need to be doing is not only

bad stewardship, but it also robs your priorities of the energy that's due them. Before you begin any task, ask yourself whether or not it's something you really need to be doing. If the answer is no, don't do it. If the answer is yes, focus on doing it efficiently. The sweet spot of time management lies at the crossroads of effectiveness and efficiency.

## 2. Pray, "God, What Is the Best Use of My Time Right Now?"

Can you imagine how effective you could become if you allowed God to direct your time? According to James, if you need wisdom about something, all you need to do is ask God, and He will give it to you (see Jas. 1:5). What if, before diving blindly into your to-do list, you were to say, "God, what's the best use of my day? What's the best use of this hour?" The goal of time management is to ensure that you are making the highest use of every day. When you ask God to direct you on what to do and when, that goal becomes much more achievable. God can make you more efficient, sure, but more importantly, He can make you efficient at being effective.

Now, let me be clear, this is not an invitation to chuck detailed planning or other time management principles. This prayer is an attitude that should cover and infuse all of your time management efforts—not an excuse to sit idly because you "didn't hear from God" on how to spend your afternoon. As you approach the work you're called to every day, choose to be open to God's guiding hand. Try writing this prayer out on a notecard or a Post-It and keeping it on your desk so that you see it several times throughout the day. Let it be a reminder to surrender the clock to God. Take the opportunity He has given you to partner with Him in crafting your time for His glory.

## 3. Adopt an Off-Peak Lifestyle

For everything you do in life, there's a peak time to do it—a time that requires more time, effort and energy—and an off-peak time. Choose

to operate in the off-peak. As a pastor, you have flexibility built into your schedule that most of the working world does not. When it comes to life's routine demands (going to the bank, the dry cleaners, the DMV, the grocery store, and the like), you don't have to keep the same schedule as the rest of the working world. You can take care of these necessities at off-peak times and therefore do them much more quickly. Once you get in the habit of living off-peak, the time you save can add up significantly. Take a look at these examples:

- *Restaurants:* What time is the lunch rush in your area? Find out and then plan your own lunchtime around it. By doing so, you can avoid sitting in traffic, having to wait for a table, and dealing with slower service—which gives you more time in your afternoon to do what you need to get done.

- *Grocery Stores:* The busiest time to go to the grocery store is right after work. Everyone is stopping by to pick up something for dinner—which means you shouldn't. Don't waste time fighting crowds and standing in long lines if you have the flexibility to run by at a slower time of the day.

- *Doctor Appointments:* Is there anything more annoying than sitting in a doctor's office waiting room for hours on end? There are certain appointment slots that can minimize your wait time. I suggest asking what those are when you make your appointment. Personally, I've found that the first appointment after lunch is the best. In the morning, doctors are busy with issues and emergencies that happened overnight. They get behind schedule fast. But no matter what, they will always come back from lunch on time. Being that first appointment when they return can cut your wait down significantly.

- *Commute:* You likely have the freedom to decide what time you get to your office and what time you leave. So why not

plan your driving time to avoid traffic? If leaving for the office an hour earlier or staying an hour later means you won't have to sit in rush-hour madness, then by all means, take advantage of the unique flexibility you have. The time adds up.

You get the picture. Simple tweaks to your routine can save you hours over the course of a month. Having a self-directed schedule is one of the benefits of working in ministry. Be sure to take advantage of it so that you can have more time for the things that matter.

---

### Renegade Pastor Testimony

As a bi-vocational pastor who works as a global manager at a Fortune 500 company, I greatly appreciate effective time management principles. When I first learned of the Renegade Pastors Network, I was skeptical about whether or not I could successfully balance it all. Now, after three years of applying the principle of living off-peak and practicing Nelson's other renegade time management principles, I have been able to grow personally, spend more time with my family, and hire our first staff person to expand the ministry.

Lawrence Williams, Lead Pastor
Lake Norman Christian Outreach—
Mooresville, North Carolina

---

## 4. Don't Start Your Day Until You've Planned Your Day

You may have heard the old axiom "Plan your work, then work your plan." The wisdom in that saying is right on point. The most productive people I know, both in ministry and otherwise, have developed a habit of planning tomorrow before they close the door on today. In other words, before they begin any new morning, they

already have a good idea of what the entire day is going to look like. They have taken time to outline the details, and then they stick to the plan they've outlined. I encourage you to do the same—and so does Solomon: "Careful planning puts you ahead in the long run; hurry and scurry puts you further behind" (Prov. 21:5, *THE MESSAGE*).

The most practical way to implement this concept is to take a few minutes every evening to prepare for the following day. (This can also help with your transition time, as discussed in Chapter 2.) Say it's Monday at 5:45 PM. Before you leave the office, spend 15 or 20 minutes sketching out what you are going to be doing on Tuesday:

- Write your to-do list.
- Make sure all of your meetings are entered into your calendar.
- Pull out the folders and documents you'll need and put them on your desk.
- Locate the tools and resources you know you'll need so that they'll be handy.

When you walk out of the office that night, walk out knowing you have done your best to be sure that Tuesday is completely planned. By doing so, you'll ensure that Tuesday runs as smoothly as possible, allowing you to be both efficient and effective with your time.

Average pastors don't do this. Having not given any thought to Tuesday on Monday night, they get to the office on Tuesday morning and wonder what they should tackle first. They hurry and scurry through the day, without following any real plan for their time, and end up more behind at the end of the day than they had been at the beginning. Can you relate? Going renegade means breaking the cycle and taking responsibility for the time God has given you to do His work.

 "The best way to predict the future is to create it."
—Peter Drucker

When you first start this practice, it won't feel natural. But over time, taking a few minutes to plan your next day will become as habitual as turning off the lights when you walk out the door. I encourage you to start immediately. Even if you can't foresee your entire day tomorrow, plan as much of it as you can. Then work that plan. The next day, try to plan a little more. Then work that plan. Soon you will be planning full days before they ever happen—and you will become more productive than you ever thought possible. (For some of my favorite planning tools, visit www.RenegadePastorBook.com.)

## 5. Develop a Top Six List

Developing a Top Six list ties into planning your day before it starts. Whether you are a list maker by nature or not, creating a to-do list of what you need to get done every day is an important part of good time management. But don't stop there. After you make your list, identify and rank the six most important tasks. When you dive into your to-do list, tackle these six tasks first, in the order you ranked them.

I'm sure you are familiar with the 80/20 Rule (also known as the Pareto Principle). The 80/20 Rule holds that 80 percent of the results in any area come from 20 percent of the work. In other words, 80 percent of your effectiveness will come from 20 percent of your focus. Developing a Top Six list allows you to harness the power of the 80/20 Rule by identifying the 20 percent (or so) of your work that will bring you the greatest return on your time. You may have 30 or 40 items on your overall list, so prioritizing the top six directs your attention to the tasks that will be most effective for your ministry.

The Top Six list also helps you move seamlessly through your day. For example, say you finish the first two items on your to-do list, but you don't have the list prioritized. You glance over the rest of the items, wondering what you should do next. At that moment of trying to prioritize on the fly, you are highly susceptible to distractions. A few minutes trying to figure out what's next can turn into

hours not doing important work, especially if you start dabbling with less pressing tasks.

On the other hand, if you finish the top two items on your to-do list and know exactly what numbers three, four, five and six are, you can keep moving forward. You can stay in a state of productivity, building momentum that will carry through the rest of your day. As you make this a habit, you'll get faster and faster at completing your Top Six list, and then you'll have more time to chip away at all of your less effective but still necessary to-dos. Again, plan your work and work your plan. You'll be able to end each day knowing you were as effective as you could be.

## 6. Eat the Frog

If you want to be a great time manager, you have to learn to enjoy the taste of frog early in the morning. In other words, you must make a habit of tackling the hardest task of the day first thing. Get it out of the way. Eat the frog. If there is something on your to-do list that you keep putting off because you dread it, move it to the number one position. Get it done so that you can focus on the other things you need to do without that one item weighing on you.

While the concept of eating the frog can be traced back to something Mark Twain said, personal effectiveness guru Brian Tracy has brought fresh light to it in his book *Eat That Frog*. He writes:

> Your "frog" is your biggest, most important task, the one you are most likely to procrastinate on if you don't do something about it. It is also the one task that can have the greatest positive impact on your life and results at the moment. . . .
>
> Think of this as a test. Treat it like a personal challenge. Resist the temptation to start with the easier task. Continually remind yourself that one of the most important decisions you make each day is what you will do immediately and what you will do later, if you do it at all. . . .

The key to reaching high levels of performance and productivity is to develop the lifelong habit of tackling your major task first thing each morning. You must develop the routine of "eating your frog" before you do anything else and without taking too much time to think about it.[2]

Sometimes eating the frog simply means diving directly into the task that is going to take the most energy and brainpower, rather than procrastinating by checking easier tasks off your list first. Sometimes it may mean having an awkward conversation with a co-worker, making an uncomfortable phone call, or writing a difficult memo. Whatever it is, getting it out of the way is crucial to your forward momentum. So, to borrow a phrase from Nike, just do it—and do it first thing.

A few years ago, someone at The Journey sent me a letter asking if we could give him a certain amount of money. Usually, I'm not involved in benevolence decisions, but for a myriad of reasons—one of which was that the letter was addressed directly to me—the letter was sitting on my desk. I knew I had to respond. After talking with a couple of staff members, we agreed that honoring the request wouldn't be a wise use of our church's resources. I needed to write the man back and decline his request, but I kept putting it off. I dreaded giving the negative response. I was afraid of what the person might think and of what he might say to other people in the church.

That live frog sat on my desk for weeks. The more I ignored it, the louder it croaked. After a while, it began to stink up my office. Every time I finished a project, I would look at that frog. I would pet it and trim its hair—and then I would move on to another project while it stared at me. Finally, one morning, I decided to eat the frog. Choking it down wasn't easy, but once it was gone, I was incredibly relieved. After I put that letter in the mail, I was able to move forward to what needed to be done next without its nagging croak ringing in my ears. These days, I have learned to enjoy the taste of frog, because I know how good eating frogs is for me. I hope you will learn to love them too.

## 7. Work in 60- to 90-Minute Blocks of Time

God has built certain rhythms into the way you live and work. Recognizing those natural rhythms and cooperating with them is key to managing your time effectively. For example, countless studies have shown that the mind is able to concentrate on one specific task for 60 to 90 minutes before needing a break. So why not use the way your brain is wired to your advantage?

Try breaking your day into several 60- to 90-minute work blocks. During each block of time, do your best to eliminate all possible distractions and focus on the task in front of you. When your block is over, you can respond to email, take phone calls, or connect with people your secretary had to hold out of your office—but during those work periods, choose to focus like a laser. Soon you'll start accomplishing more and more in each block. This simple time organization tool will increase your productivity exponentially.

## 8. Work All the Time You're at Work

Think back to the boundaries discussion in Chapter 2. In the same way that you put boundary lines around certain areas of your family life in order to bring health and harmony to your relationships, you should also draw those lines around your ministry. One of those boundaries is committing to work all the time you are at work. Some studies show that during an 8-hour workday, the average person only works 2 hours. If you want to quadruple your efficiency, learn to use the full 8 or 10 hours of your workday for work. Intentionally eliminate distractions that can keep you from being focused on the tasks God has put in front of you.

You may have heard the classic story about the busy executive with a new wife and baby at home. Whenever he was at work, he felt guilty that he wasn't spending enough time at home. His mind was constantly on his wife and newborn. But when he got home, he was consumed with all that needed to be done at work. Because he had been ineffective at the office during the day, he would worry about the deals he

needed to move along and the paperwork that was piling up on his desk. This poor guy never got anything done or fully connected with his family, because he couldn't master the simple principle of working while he was at work. If he had, he could have been more effective on the job and been able to connect more deeply while he was at home.

When you get to the office in the morning, switch your mind into work mode. Eat the frog. Start tackling your Top Six list. Work your 60- to 90-minute blocks. Discipline yourself to focus on your work while you are at work. As you do these things, you will be free to enjoy the other parts of your life when the day is done.

## 9. Learn to Delegate

Control is a trap that will keep you from growing. When you try to control everything, you quickly become overwhelmed and stressed out—not to mention, you rob both yourself and others of the opportunity to evolve. If you want to be healthy and continue progressing, you must learn to delegate. As a leader, it's a skill you can't afford to be without. Good delegation is essential on two levels:

1. The worst thing, in terms of managing your time, is doing something that doesn't need to be done at all. The next worst thing is doing something that someone else should be doing. As you approach the to-dos on your list, get in the habit of asking yourself, *Is this something I should be doing, or is this something I should delegate?* Shakespeare may have written, "To be or not to be? That is the question." But when it comes to your time, ask, "To do or not to do?" That should be the real question.

2. Part of your calling as a pastor is to equip others to do the work of ministry (see Eph. 4:11-12). People learn by doing. In order to equip those whom you are leading, you have to trust them enough to hand responsibility

over to them. You have to be willing to let go—but that doesn't mean you don't have a system in place for overseeing what you delegate. When you delegate:

- Be clear about what you want done. After you explain what needs to be done, have the person you are delegating to repeat the request back to you.
- Agree to a timeline for completion.
- Have a feedback loop in place. That is, set an expectation that your delegate will get in touch with you when he is finished with the task. Then, evaluate the work and give him feedback.

If you ever catch yourself thinking, *If you want something done right, just do it yourself,* you're headed for trouble. While that mindset is valued in our culture, it's poison for leaders who are trying to manage their time well, equip disciples for ministry, and be effective for God's Kingdom. (For my top resources on delegation, visit www. RenegadePastorBook.com.)

## 10. Practice the Sabbath

I have a confession to make. About two years after I started The Journey, around the time our New York City location really began to grow, I was living in sin. I had been living in sin for years, actually, unashamedly violating the Fourth Commandment:

Remember to observe the Sabbath day by keeping it holy. You have six days each week for your ordinary work, but the seventh day is a Sabbath day of rest dedicated to the LORD your God (Exod. 20:8-10).

On a day I'll never forget, a mentor in my life confronted me about this issue. He called me a sinner for continuing to violate the

Sabbath. He said that not only was I sabotaging my marriage and ruining my health, but God also wouldn't be able to bless my church anymore if I didn't start taking a day off. At first, I was furious. After all, I was doing what needed to be done to keep my ministry afloat. I didn't have time to rest. How dare he call me a sinner when I was dedicating every waking hour to building God's church? But after I calmed down, I realized he was right—and his willingness to call me out ultimately saved my ministry.

The Sabbath is the key to future ministry viability. It's essential for keeping your relationship with your spouse and family strong, and for keeping yourself physically, emotionally and spiritually healthy. Above all else, honoring the Sabbath is crucial to maintaining a close relationship with God. God didn't slip the Sabbath into the Ten Commandments simply because He thought some time off each week would be a good idea; He understood that continual work without regular periods of release would destroy His creation. As Charles Spurgeon put it:

> Even beasts of burden must be turned out to grass occasionally. The very sea pauses at ebb and flood. Earth keeps the Sabbath of the wintery months, and man, even when exalted to be God's ambassador, must rest or faint, must trim his lamp or let it burn low, must recruit his vigor or grow prematurely old. . . . In the long run, we shall do more by sometimes doing less.[3]

The Sabbath is more than a time management practice. It is inextricably connected to the first three commitments of being a renegade pastor: (1) follow your Lord, (2) love your family, and (3) fulfill your calling. You cannot do those three things with any level of excellence without obeying God's command to honor the Sabbath.

The Sabbath is a 24-hour period dedicated to God as an offering every 7 days. Which 24-hour period it is doesn't matter; any 24 hours will do. Obviously, your Sabbath isn't going to be on Sunday. A common

Sabbath time for pastors is sundown on Friday to sundown on Saturday. Or you may want to take your Sabbath on a Tuesday. The day is irrelevant; what matters is your willingness to spend 24 hours apart from all ministry work. For one full day, relinquish control of the universe back to its rightful owner. Choosing to step away, no matter how busy you are or what's going on, proves your trust in God's control.

Have you ever had anyone tell you they don't have enough money to tithe? What is your response? My guess is something along the lines of: "Trust God and tithe. You'll see that He's faithful to provide." The reality behind taking a Sabbath is strikingly similar. When people tithe, they quickly discover that they have an easier time living on 90 percent of their income than they did living on 100 percent. When you choose to honor the Sabbath, you realize that you can get more done in six days with one day of rest than you can working all seven—and with more peace, less stress and greater effectiveness. When you give Him one day, He blesses the other six more abundantly. Tithing hinges on God's math; the Sabbath hinges on His calendar. Trust God and take a day off.

Part of my original problem with taking a Sabbath, in addition to thinking I didn't have the time, was that I didn't know what to do with myself if I wasn't working. I couldn't imagine taking a day away from ministry work to do . . . nothing. But as I quickly learned, the Sabbath is not about idling. There are four important elements to an effective Sabbath: Rest, Reflection, Recreation and Proflection.

*Rest*—Rest can be either passive or active. Passive rest is sleeping or lounging around the house not doing much. While there is a time for that, it's not how you should spend your whole Sabbath. If you need to catch up on some sleep, by all means do. But then engage in more active rest. That is, do something restful that grows and renews you. Maybe you want to spend more time reading on your Sabbath than you usually have time for. Maybe you're a big fan of crossword puzzles, so you spend an hour challenging your brain. Whatever it is that works for you, engage in some restful activity.

*Reflection*—Take time on the Sabbath to look back over the last six days and evaluate how things went. Thank God for what went well. Practice intentional gratefulness. Also take a hard look at the things that didn't go well. The Sabbath is the perfect time to hit the reset button if something hasn't been going the way you want it to go. God is giving you the opportunity to fix whatever's not working before you plunge ahead into the next week.

One exercise I personally engage in on my Sabbath is to think through the fruit of the Spirit and reflect on how well I did with each one over the previous week. How well did I love? Did I keep peace or did I lose my temper? You get the idea. Don't miss the opportunity the Sabbath is giving you to evaluate yourself and your ministry through God's eyes. Think deeply in His presence. That, by the way, is my favorite definition of prayer: Prayer, in its essence, is thinking deeply in the presence of God.

*Recreation*—If you break down the word "recreation," you get re-creation. Your Sabbath is a good day to re-create yourself and the relationships in your life. Think about how you can use your Sabbath to reconnect with your spouse or with your children. Schedule time with friends you don't get to see often or reach out to your parents. This is the perfect day to nurture your relationships with the people you love.

*Proflection*—I made up the word "proflection." It simply means to think about the future. Spend time on your Sabbath thinking through the next six days, the next six weeks, or even the next six months. This ties into the time management practice mentioned above: Don't start your day until you've planned your day. The Sabbath gives you an opportunity to do some planning. As you engage in prayerful proflection, God may begin to change what you will do over the next six days. You may begin to focus on higher-level activities simply because you've allowed yourself the opportunity to pull away, rest and spend time with Him. (For information on godly goal setting, visit www. RenegadePastorBook.com.)

I know you're a pastor; so am I. You have heard a lot of this before; so had I. You even teach on keeping the Sabbath; so did I. But I wasn't practicing what I preached, and it almost destroyed me. How about

you? Are you living in sin when it comes to honoring the Sabbath? (For more on keeping the Sabbath, download my resource, *The Power of the Sabbath*, at www.RenegadePastorBook.com.)

## The Time of Your Life

If you have spent much time visiting the dying in hospitals or nursing homes, you've had an up-close, personal view of a reality most people don't like to take to heart. Time eventually runs out. Life in this world ends. When it does, the nearly universal desire is for more of it. Men and women facing the end of their lives would give anything to have just a few more healthy days with the people they love, doing what they were called to do, before taking that step into heaven.

King David writes, "Teach us to number our days, that we may gain a heart of wisdom" (Ps. 90:12, *NIV*). To paraphrase, I believe he is saying, "Keep us mindful that there's a deadline—there's an end to our life on earth—so that we will approach our time with wisdom." When you are able to live in light of the fact that your time here is limited, the share you have of it becomes more valuable. As a result, you become committed to spending it differently.

In God's eyes, your entire life is shorter than that week before vacation. Before you can turn around, it will be Thursday afternoon. Shouldn't you do all you can to manage what you've been given to the best of your ability? Remembering that there is a deadline on your earthly existence will help you to appreciate every moment, focusing on how you can leverage this precious resource for your benefit and for God's glory before you jet off into eternity. (For more information on making the highest use of your time, see my complete treatment in the resource *Time Management for Busy Pastors* at www.RenegadePastorBook.com.)

| Renegade Pastor Testimony |
| --- |

When I started with the Renegade Pastors Network, I had six small children at home, and I was overwhelmed by the

demands. The network taught me to make marriage and family a priority and to take time off as an act of faith. I learned that the worst use of time is to do something really well that doesn't need to be done at all. Over the past few years of being in the network, my church has grown exponentially. I have more time with my wife and family than ever before—and my family has grown to include five more children.

Dan Plourde, Pastor
Calvary Church—Jupiter, Florida

# *Commitment Five:* Shepherd Your Flock

*Demystifying Your Job Description*

A preacher must be both soldier and shepherd. He must
nourish, defend, and teach; he must have teeth
in his mouth, and be able to bite and fight.

MARTIN LUTHER

He will feed his flock like a shepherd. He will carry the
lambs in his arms, holding them close to his heart.

ISAIAH 40:11

Going renegade is all about learning to stand in the tradition of Christianity's boldest, most influential leaders—like the apostle Peter. But as I'm sure you know, Peter's story didn't always seem so promising. After vowing never to desert Jesus, Peter denied knowing Him three times in the same night (see Matt. 26:33-34,69-75). Understandably, he was disgusted with himself. Dejected and feeling like a failure, Peter went back to his old way of living as soon as Jesus was crucified. He decided that average would be good enough for him, and he returned to the life of a fisherman. But Jesus still had other plans in mind for the future renegade. After His resurrection, Jesus paid a visit to Peter and the other disciples who were with him:

At dawn Jesus was standing on the beach, but the disciples couldn't see who he was. He called out, "Fellows, have you caught any fish?"

"No," they replied.

Then he said, "Throw out your net on the right-hand side of the boat, and you'll get some!" So they did, and they couldn't haul in the net because there were so many fish in it.

Then the disciple Jesus loved said to Peter, "It's the Lord!" When Simon Peter heard that it was the Lord, he put on his tunic (for he had stripped for work), jumped into the water, and headed to shore. The others stayed with the boat and pulled the loaded net to the shore, for they were only about a hundred yards from shore. When they got there, they found breakfast waiting for them—fish cooking over a charcoal fire, and some bread.

"Bring some of the fish you've just caught," Jesus said. So Simon Peter went aboard and dragged the net to the shore. There were 153 large fish, and yet the net hadn't torn.

"Now come and have some breakfast!" Jesus said. None of the disciples dared to ask him, "Who are you?" They knew it was the Lord. Then Jesus served them the bread and the fish. This was the third time Jesus had appeared to his disciples since he had been raised from the dead.

After breakfast Jesus asked Simon Peter, "Simon son of John, do you love me more than these?"

"Yes, Lord," Peter replied, "you know I love you."

"Then feed my lambs," Jesus told him.

Jesus repeated the question: "Simon son of John, do you love me?"

"Yes, Lord," Peter said, "you know I love you."

"Then take care of my sheep," Jesus said.

A third time he asked him, "Simon son of John, do you love me?"

Peter was hurt that Jesus asked the question a third time.

He said, "Lord, you know everything. You know that I love you."

Jesus said, "Then feed my sheep" (John 21:4-17).

In that moment, Peter was restored. His denials were negated, and he stood with a new call on his life—a call to shepherd the flock Jesus would lead into his care. Peter went on to do just that, becoming a cornerstone leader of the emerging Christian movement.

In the Holy Land, a small church has been built on the edge of the Sea of Galilee, where the exchange between Jesus and Peter took place. Whenever I visit, I make a point of stopping by early in the morning and spending some time on the shore in the spot of that famous breakfast meeting. Standing there, I'm always filled with awe that God has given me the same mission He gave Peter—the mission to feed His sheep. The responsibility that began with Peter has been passed through generation after generation of pastors for thousands of years and now rests squarely on my shoulders. But I'm not the only one; it rests just as squarely on yours.

 ### Renegade Commitment Five: Shepherd Your Flock

God has entrusted a flock of sheep to you. They may be lost sheep; they may be black sheep; some may bite; some will follow your lead without much question, while others will be stubborn. No matter, they are yours. You have a responsibility to shepherd them well. God has deemed you worthy of their care. He has handpicked you to point them toward salvation and disciple them along the way. These aren't tasks that can be taken lightly. You have been given an assignment to shepherd your flock with an excellence that reflects the love and glory of God—to shepherd them in the same renegade way ultimately modeled by Peter as he preached on the day of Pentecost, led the church in Jerusalem, and penned two powerful New Testament epistles that help define the role of a pastor. As you choose to intentionally shepherd your flock the way

Jesus intends, you'll be fulfilling the fifth commitment of being a renegade pastor.

Enter the confusion and debate. While the concept of shepherding a flock may seem straightforward on the surface, there is a lot of uncertainty swirling through pastoral circles about the best, most biblical way to care for the people you've been entrusted with. This issue is too important to muddle through; after all, one day God will hold you accountable for what kind of job you've done. The key to demystifying your role as a shepherd is to acknowledge and start focusing on the three most critical tasks you've been called to fulfill as a pastor: (1) lead your sheep, (2) feed your sheep, and (3) protect your sheep.

## Lead Your Sheep

When you stepped into the role of pastor, you immediately became a leader, whether you were prepared to be one or not. Not only are you responsible for guiding the day-to-day operations of your church and your staff toward the vision God has given you, but you are also charged with leading the sheep you've been given—no matter how few or how many they may be. There are four key components to leading well: You must (1) continue learning, (2) be eager to engage, (3) be quick to anticipate, and (4) make wise decisions. Of course there's a handy acronym to help you remember these four tenets of leadership: Learn, Engage, Anticipate, Decide. Here's more detail on each:

First, leaders are learners. Remember our discussion about the importance of creating a personal growth plan in Chapter 3? To recap, your church's growth will never healthily outpace your personal growth. If you want to lead a growing congregation full of growing people, you have to decide to be a lifelong student of your calling. You need to commit to the reading plan outlined earlier and take the time to get yourself around other likeminded leaders. Keep going deeper in your knowledge of what it takes to partner with God in creating a healthy church so that your people have the best

opportunity to become fully developing followers of Jesus. (More on creating a healthy church in Chapter 6.) If you aren't continually learning, you will put a self-imposed cap on your ability to shepherd your flock toward the pastures God intends for them.

What Does a Leader Do?
**L**earns
**E**ngages
**A**nticipates
**D**ecides

Second, leaders are eager to engage with their people. I bet you know pastors who have gotten so burnt out that they become distant both from their staff and from their flock. Sometimes they will even hire a go-between, such as an executive pastor, so that they don't have to spend as much time in the trenches, dealing with problems and issues. While there's nothing wrong with hiring help and changing the focus of your workload at various points in the life of your church, you can never let that cause you to disengage. Stay among the people. Otherwise, you'll lose your feel for the pulse of your congregation.

One of the most important aspects of staying engaged is to stay on top of any potential conflict. As I've already mentioned, you should be prepared to run to conflict. Catch it in its earliest stages, before it has a chance to spread. If you don't, it will splinter out of control and create multitudes of problems that could have been avoided with a little pro-activity.

Have you ever been driving along, minding your own business, when a rock pops up and hits your windshield? The small chip it creates is annoying, sure, but not much of a problem. It's a quick and easy fix; any auto glass repair shop can fill the chip with glue and, like magic, it disappears. But if you don't take the time to fix it early on, you know what happens. The chip starts to grow. Cracks start splintering out in every direction. The longer you ignore it, the worse it gets. Eventually, if the situation is left unaddressed,

your whole windshield will be destroyed. The same reality applies to conflict in your church. If you address issues in their earliest stages, you can keep them from spreading and causing irreparable damage. Stay engaged with your people and meet problems head on, before they splinter out and create major issues.

 "Leadership is anticipation."—Steve Stroope

Third, leaders anticipate. One of my mentors, Steve Stroope, likes to say, "Leadership is anticipation." As a leader, you should always be thinking five steps ahead of everyone else. Keep an eye toward what's coming down the pike in every area of your church so that you'll be less likely to be caught off guard by anything. Anticipate what the budget is going to be next year and plan accordingly now. Anticipate what the preaching calendar will be and what new needs may start arising in your small-group system. The ability to anticipate is what separates average leaders from excellent leaders.

Finally, leaders are deciders. You have to make decisions that are in the best interest of your flock, which is not always as easy as it sounds. Start by praying over the decision you need to make. Then seek out what the Bible has to say. Next, look to any existing historical precedent. That is, consider how others have handled the same type of decision or situation. After you've done those three things, seek out the advice of others. You can get into trouble if you skip to seeking input from others before looking for God's leading first.

Once you've made a decision, stay engaged to be sure the decision is implemented properly. There's something to be said for making right decisions, but there's even more to be said for making decisions rightly. In other words, see those choices through to make sure they are executed correctly. A mediocre decision that's well implemented is far better than a great decision that's poorly implemented.

 A mediocre decision that's well implemented is far better than a great decision that's poorly implemented.

As you think through these four tenets of strong leadership (**L**earn, **E**ngage, **A**nticipate, **D**ecide), keep your responsibility to your people squarely in mind. They are your flock; you are their shepherd. You can't forego your call to leadership by turning their growth and well-being over to staff or to high-level laity in your church. Now, I'm not saying you can't delegate. You should. Delegation is a crucial skill, as detailed in Chapter 4. But even when you delegate specific tasks and areas of leadership to your under-shepherds, the responsibility for your sheep is still on you. There are three areas in particular where it pays to be intentionally diligent about stepping fully into your God-given leadership role: (1) stewardship, (2) evangelism, and (3) ministry.

## Stewardship

God has put a specific plan in place to resource His church and to lead His people out of financial repression. You carry a large part of the impetus for bringing that plan about. Teaching your people biblical stewardship principles is part of shepherding them well. You can't just step back and hope they'll give. There are specific steps you need to take to help release the strongholds the enemy wants to have on their finances.

Take the lead by educating your people on the biblical basis of stewardship during your weekend service. The majority of your congregation probably has no idea what the Bible says about giving—and many of those who think they do know are misinformed. As long as your people remain ignorant on the topic, they won't have a fair opportunity to grow into godly stewards—or into fully developing disciples, for that matter. You can spearhead the charge by teaching on stewardship, incorporating stewardship testimonies into your services, and issuing giving challenges.

*Stewardship Teaching—Four Times Per Year:* Adopt the same boldness Jesus had in teaching on money and possessions. He understood that a person's heart is tied directly to his or her checkbook. Given His interest in hearts, Jesus had no choice but to take a strong stand on money matters; neither do you. I suggest teaching on stewardship at least four times every year, as follows:

- *Mid to Late January*—Strategically speaking, you should plan the first stewardship message of the year around the second or third weekend of January. Your people will be recovering from the Christmas rush. Bills will be coming in. They are going to be thinking about what the year ahead holds and what kinds of changes they need to make. This is a perfect time to teach on issues of budgeting, debt, and how to get your financial house in order.

- *Right After Back-to-School*—The beginning of the school year is the other natural period when people pause to reorganize their lives. There are new schedules and new routines. Depending on the part of the country you are in, this may be in August or September. Whatever the actual date, just make sure you plan the teaching for a week or two after everyone gets into the swing of the fall schedule so that the majority of your regular attenders will be there.

The other two stewardship Sundays during the year are up to your discretion. I usually like to do something around Easter and then revisit the topic over the summer. Feel out what works best with the flow of your calendar. What's most important is not when you preach on money, but that you take the lead and do it.

*Stewardship Testimonies—Two Times Per Year:* Let your people hear from someone in the church who has struggled with finances and has seen the blessings that come with deciding to honor God despite the struggle. Let them hear from someone who could be considered wealthy, but who has learned the truth about want versus need and how to live with a heart toward God's abundance. The greater the variety of testimonies you offer, the greater the number of people who will be influenced. I suggest scheduling short stewardship testimonies at least two times every year. At The Journey, we usually keep testimonies to four minutes or less. That's all it takes to touch someone's heart in a powerful way.

*Giving Challenges—Two Times Per Year:* Human beings are wired to respond to challenges. One of the most effective ways to lead your people to give is to boldly challenge them to start giving. I suggest putting forth giving challenges at least twice every year. (Much more detail on giving challenges will be shared later in this chapter.)

Now, while you are the chief fundraiser for your church, that doesn't mean you need to be the church accountant. In fact, I suggest you have someone else handle the actual number crunching. But you do need to know what's going on. You have to provide vision and accountability. You should get periodic reports on the financial status of the church. Make sure you know your weekly, monthly and quarterly budget needs and how giving is matching up to those. Don't step back and let others lead in this area just because it may make you a little uncomfortable. You don't have to run everything, but you do have to take the lead in discipling your people toward stewardship and stay involved in the details.

The number one reason pastors are afraid to step up and take a leadership role when it comes to money is that they don't have personal integrity with their own. The first step to being able to lead your church financially is getting your own finances in order. If you aren't faithfully tithing, start. Make a decision to get out of debt and begin living within your means. When you are honoring God's plan for your money, you will be better able to lead your people into doing the same. (For an in-depth examination of how to create a strong stewardship system, see my book *Maximize: How to Develop Extravagant Givers in Your Church.*[1])

## Evangelism

As the pastor, it is your job to keep the evangelistic temperature of your church boiling hot. It doesn't matter whether you are a gifted evangelist or not. You may have someone else in your church who loves evangelism so much that you are tempted to turn over the reins. Don't do it. You must lead.

Accepting your proper leadership role in the area of evangelism is the only hope you have of keeping your church focused on reaching

others for Jesus. Your people will head in the direction you point them. You can effectively direct them toward evangelism in three ways: (1) through the stage, (2) through your staff, and (3) through structure.

*Stage*: Every Sunday you are given an opportunity. There are points in the service you can take advantage of to raise the value of what's important. Your strategic use of sermons, challenges (again, more on challenges in the next section), announcements, and vision casting from the stage can raise the level of evangelism in your church more quickly than anything else. Here are some things to try:

- *Personal Stories*—The best way to create a heart for evangelism in your people is to share your personal evangelism stories. There's power in being able to say, "You know, last week when I was sharing my faith with someone . . ." or "Yesterday when I invited my neighbor to church . . ." As soon as you begin telling a story from your own life, it's like you've just picked up a megaphone. The key here is that you have to have these stories to tell. If you aren't reaching out to the unchurched, then you can't talk about evangelism with integrity.

- *Testimonies*—At appropriate times, have people tell their stories of evangelism from the stage. When your people see their peers reaching others for Jesus, they will have more faith that they can do the same.

- *Preaching*—Plan evangelism messages into your preaching calendar. For example, every three years, I teach an entire sermon series on evangelism. Every three years, I also teach an entire series on stewardship and one on ministry. I can't teach a series on evangelism, one on stewardship and one on ministry every year. But this three-year plan ensures that, at least once every three years, my congregation gets a four- to five-week series on the ins and outs of evangelism. (For more information on developing your preaching calendar,

go to www.RenegadePastorBook.com.) In addition, I work smaller evangelism pushes into various sermons throughout the year, every year, in the ways mentioned above.

- *Immediate Opportunities for Action*—If you have just preached a message on evangelism, make sure you give your people an immediate opportunity to live out what they've learned. Say it's Palm Sunday and you have preached a passionate message about the importance of inviting people to church for Easter. Back that up by providing a way to act. Have invitation cards printed before the service and give each person four or five cards as they leave. They can use those cards as a tool to invite people to the Easter service. You are making it easier for them to take immediate action.

*Staff:* In order to lead in the area of evangelism, you have to expect a high level of evangelistic involvement from your staff—and you have to hold them accountable to those expectations. I would encourage you to make a heart for evangelism one of the standard prerequisites for all new hires. Make sure your staff members are serving in evangelistic activities, praying for their unchurched friends, and inviting those friends to big days at your church.

*Structure:* Take a minute to think about the underlying structure of your church as it relates to evangelism. Have you structured for growth? Have you structured with an eye toward the greater community? Have you structured in a way that helps you mobilize your people for evangelism? Here are three ways you can make sure you are constantly raising the evangelistic temperature of your church through your structure:

- *Plan Regular Evangelistic Events*—Make sure your evangelistic events aren't makeshift. Plan them well in advance. Start putting the word out long before the date of the event. If you haven't been doing many outreach activities, don't let

the idea intimidate you. Just make a decision to get started. Plan a carwash, a family picnic or a prayer walk. Decide on an event or two and get them on the calendar.

- *Engage Small Groups in Evangelism*—From time to time, encourage your small groups to do a mini-study on evangelism as a part of their regular semester. Have group members read a book on sharing their faith and challenge them to hold one another accountable for doing so. Taking two or three weeks to underscore the importance of evangelism and to give your small-group members some tools for reaching out is well worth the effort and planning.

- *Structure for Celebration*—Build opportunities into your church's structure for consistently celebrating evangelism. At The Journey, we always videotape our baptism celebrations, complete with brief testimonies from the people who are being baptized, and then edit the footage into a two- or three-minute piece to be shown in a weekend service. We want everyone to see the celebration of life change that is happening as a result of our willingness to reach out.

Inevitably, several of the people being baptized say something along the lines of, "I hadn't been to church in years and then my friend from school invited me to come with him," or "I was just walking down the street one day and this girl gave me an invitation to her church. It was at just the right time because I had really been struggling." When the congregation hears these stories, they get excited about the evidence of changed lives. That gives them a renewed sense of the power of evangelism. And up goes the level of evangelism in your church.

By making sure you are doing your part to keep the evangelistic temperature of your church hot, you are saying to God, *I am ready and willing to hold up my end of this deal. I will lead. I will shepherd my flock to be passionate for evangelism so that You might work through*

*us to draw people into Your Kingdom.* (For more on keeping the evangelistic temperature in your church at the boiling point, see *Ignite: How to Spark Immediate Growth in Your Church*[2] and go to www. RenegadePastorBook.com.)

## Ministry

God wants all of your people to be actively engaged, serving in an area of ministry He has gifted them for. Your job is to help each person identify and get plugged into a volunteer role where he or she can flourish and the church can benefit. If you fail to connect your people to significant ministry, you are robbing them of the opportunity to grow—and that's not what a faithful shepherd does. Again, while you may have other staff members or high-capacity laity heading up various areas of ministry, you are the ultimate leader. You have to take the lead on getting people plugged in. Here are a few practical tactics for connecting more volunteers:

*Preach on ministry and serving:* Ministry simply means to serve. Do your members and attenders understand the biblical imperative to serve? Part of involving people in the work of the church is making sure they get the *why* behind it. Plan to teach a message on servanthood at least three times every year. I suggest scheduling one ministry-oriented message in January, one pre-summer and one pre-fall. These are the three time periods when people are most likely to take a new step and get more involved. In addition, do an entire four- to six-week sermon series on ministry every three years, as I mentioned above.

*Tie serving to membership and to small groups, and hold people accountable:* You probably have a membership covenant and a small-group covenant in place at your church. You know, documents people sign when they join the church or join a small group, respectively. If you don't, I highly recommend putting such covenants in place. Covenants create clarity. They let people know what is expected of them and give you the ability to hold your members accountable to those expectations. Take a look at our membership covenant and small-group covenant.

## Membership Covenant

1. **I will protect the unity of my church . . .**
   by acting in love toward other members
   by refusing to gossip
   by following the leaders

2. **I will share the responsibility of my church . . .**
   by praying for its growth
   by inviting the unchurched to attend
   by warmly welcoming those who visit

3. **I will serve the ministry of my church . . .**
   by discovering my gifts and talents
   by being equipped to serve by my pastors
   by developing a servant's heart

4. **I will support the testimony of my church . . .**
   by attending faithfully
   by living a godly life
   by giving regularly

Signature: _____

Date: _____

* For a free electronic version of this covenant, visit www.RenegadePastorBook.com.

## *The Journey Growth Group Covenant*

Welcome to Growth Groups at The Journey. Congratulations on your desire to grow deeper in your relationship with God through this weekly study and the relationships that will begin in this Growth Group.

As a member of this group, you will be asked to enter into a covenant with the other members to make this Growth Group a priority. To be a part of the group, you are asked to make the following commitments:

1. I will make this group a priority by attending each week, keeping up with my assignments and participating in group discussion.

2. I will regularly attend The Journey services and contribute to the ministry of the church through my attendance, giving, service and inviting of others.

3. I will strive to build authentic relationships with those in this group by showing care, providing encouragement and praying for their needs.

4. I will serve together with my group once a month during the semester and will participate in a mission project and play together with my group at least once.

5. I will explore honestly my next steps for spiritual growth.

Signature: _____

Date: _____

* For a free electronic version of this covenant, visit www.RenegadePastorBook.com.

Notice that both the membership covenant and the small-group covenant call people to serve. Because each member and small-group participant has signed at least one of the above covenants (most have signed both), they are all accountable for what the covenant contains. If I notice that one of our members has never served, or has become uninvolved in serving for a substantial period of time, I give that person a call to make sure everything is okay. I can also use the call to steer the wayward sheep back into ministry.

Small groups are a phenomenal way for people to take a first step into serving. As you see in the small-group covenant, all of our group members are required to volunteer with their group during at least one Sunday service per semester. In general, our people get involved with a group before they start serving. As a result, approximately 70 percent of our new servers take their first step into serving thanks to this small-group commitment. While they are there, we take some time to talk to them about the significance of serving, sign them up to serve again, and encourage them to get involved in serving regularly.

*Make it easy for people to sign up to serve*: Signing up should be a simple, streamlined process. I've been in churches where signing up to serve seemed harder than filling out tax forms. Keep it simple. How much information do you really need from someone who wants to work the refreshment table or volunteer in the office? A name, address and valid driver's license should be sufficient. The one exception to this rule is your children's ministry. When it comes to screening volunteers to work with children, I suggest running a full background check. You need to be extra careful with the people to whom you entrust your attenders' children.

*Ask not, "How few do we need?" but rather, "How many can we mobilize?"*: When it comes to volunteers, the average pastor's way of thinking goes something like this: *Well, we really need three ushers this week to make sure things run smoothly. I guess we could get by with two. Lord, please send us two people!* Instead of operating out of that scarcity mentality, why not think in terms of abundance? Forget the

four-letter word *need*, and ask yourself how many people you can mobilize. I would have three ushers per row every weekend if I could mobilize that many people. Think big. Lead big. (For an in-depth study on mobilizing your people for ministry, see *Connect: How to Double Your Number of Volunteers.*[3])

---

### *Renegade Pastor Testimony*

I had become extremely frustrated in my ministry. I was overwhelmed with all I was doing and needed to be doing. After entering coaching with Nelson, I realized what was going on—I thought I knew what I should be doing, but I didn't. My members were telling me what they thought I should do, but I had failed to listen to what God wanted me to do. Nelson helped me achieve clarity about my responsibilities as a pastor. I received encouragement as a leader and the tools to fulfill the tasks necessary for leading my church well. I am learning to be the leader God has called me to be and to lead my church to being above average.

George Price, Lead Pastor
First United Methodist Church—Childress, Texas

---

## Feed Your Sheep

Not only do you need to lead the flock God has called you to shepherd, but you must also feed them. Feeding your flock includes teaching them the Bible, leading them to pray, and getting them involved in small groups with other believers. Plus, as a shepherd, it's important for you to help your sheep learn to feed themselves. If you do your job well, they will know how to study the Bible on their own; engage in powerful, personal conversation with God; and seek out additional truth and teaching throughout the week.

One of the greatest, most under-utilized tools for feeding your flock is to issue challenges to them. Often, sheep don't get sufficient nutrition because they are too sluggish to eat. They become bored and lackadaisical, which leads to apathy. You don't want apathetic sheep. Challenges keep them connected and hungry. Challenges spur discipleship by engaging them in the disciplines God has called them to. Here's how you can use challenges to feed your people in the three critical areas of stewardship, evangelism and ministry:

## Stewardship

A giving challenge is an ideal way to get hesitant sheep to commit to giving for a specified period of time and to re-engage those who may have fallen off. The best way to introduce a giving challenge is to tie it in with one of your messages or testimonies on stewardship. Turn your people's attention to the idea of honoring God through their finances, and then immediately encourage them to begin giving. The key is to attach a timeframe to the challenge. Dare them to trust God and commit to giving for two months, four months or six months—whatever length you want. By the time the challenge is over, God will have proven Himself faithful to honor their giving and they won't want to stop.

Let me tell you one of my favorite stories. It's about the first true tithe challenge we ever did at The Journey. During the second message of a four-part series on stewardship, we decided to really hit hard on the importance of bringing the full tithe to God. My executive pastor started the message by talking about the history of the tithe and about how God deserves our best rather than our leftovers. Then I came out to do the second part of the message and laid out the tithe challenge. I barely even mentioned giving for the first time or regular giving. Instead, I shot right to the heart of the issue and let everyone know they should be tithing.

My goal was to challenge everyone in the congregation to commit to tithing for four months. This message was delivered in September, so I was asking them to faithfully give the first 10 percent of their income

for September, October, November and December. I knew that, if they agreed, by the end of the four months, the tithe would be a regular part of their lives, and God would be showing Himself to them in a very real way. I called on them to be serious about their growth. I called on them to be the people God had created them to be. By the time I finished issuing the challenge, I had set the bar pretty high. I was hoping that at least 40 or 50 people would be willing to jump over it. Fifty new tithers would really have been something to celebrate.

Are you ready for this? By the end of that day's services, more than 300 people had committed to the tithe challenge. I was eager to lead 50 people into God's plan for stewardship but, as usual, His vision was bigger than mine. The next Sunday, I talked about the challenge again. I thanked those who had signed up and gave people another opportunity to jump on board. Another hundred people took the challenge. All in all, we ended up with just over 400 people committed to our four-month tithe challenge.

Did that many people take the challenge because of my eloquence and brilliant articulation on the principle of tithing? Absolutely not. All I did was try my best to feed my sheep the truth about giving, make that truth relevant to their lives, and call them to action. People want to grow; they respond to well-presented challenges that will help them honor God with their lives. Part of feeding them is being willing to step out of your comfort zone and challenge your people to step out of theirs. (For more on issuing a tithe challenge, see the resources at www.RenegadePastorBook.com.)

## Evangelism

Challenging your people to pray for their unchurched friends and invite them to church is also a powerful way to feed them. In Colossians 4:2-3, Paul writes:

> Devote yourselves to prayer with an alert mind and a thankful heart. Pray for us, too, that God will give us many opportunities to speak about His mysterious plan concerning Christ.

God wants to give people opportunities to share their faith. He may already be putting those opportunities in front of your sheep, but if you aren't training them to see the open doors, they won't. Start by simply challenging them to get in the habit of praying for the people in their lives who don't know Jesus. As they pray for those individuals, their hearts will be drawn to them. Then, encourage them to invite those same people to church. As your people respond to evangelism challenges, God will open new doors of opportunity for them and help make them aware of the ones that are already open.

At The Journey, we issue the same challenge every single Sunday. After each service, we say, "If you found today's message helpful, why not invite a friend to join you next week?" If I know that an upcoming sermon's topic is going to be aimed at a widespread felt-need, I'll mention that. "Hey, next week, we are going to be talking about dealing with stress in marriage. If you know someone who might find that message helpful, bring that person with you." Keep repeating your challenge; your people will step up.

To take things further, we also use an Invest and Invite card—a business-sized card that says, on one side: "I will seek to invest in others who don't have a personal relationship with Jesus Christ and invite them to The Journey." On the other side, there are three lines for our people to list the names of three friends they are committing to invest in and invite to church. We encourage everyone to keep this card in use throughout the year. If one of the friends on the list moves away, we want them to add another friend's name. As part of continually challenging my flock, I always lead people to fill out a new Invest and Invite card when we have a special day approaching. (To see and download Invest and Invite card samples, go to www. RenegadePastorBook.com.)

## Ministry

You are the head volunteer recruiter for your church. Step up and challenge your flock to serve. Always be on the lookout for ways to get people involved—both in regular, ongoing ministry opportunities

and with one-time challenges that get new people on board. Never waste an opportunity to get people connected to ministry. For example, you can leverage big days and special events to get people to volunteer. Many of those in your church who aren't currently serving would be more willing to serve on an especially important day or for a special event than for a normal weekend service. So, when anything out of the ordinary is happening, invite new volunteers to be a part of it.

Several years ago, The Journey was meeting at a performance center in midtown Manhattan. The venue had two main theaters—an upstairs theater and a downstairs theater—and we usually met upstairs. But every once in a while, the venue would book something upstairs on a Sunday, and we would have to meet in the downstairs theater instead. Technically, this wasn't a big deal for us. In some ways it was easier to set up downstairs than upstairs. But every time the venue asked us to move for a week, I leveraged the opportunity to try to get new people to serve.

I would send an email to people in our church who weren't currently involved in serving and say, "Hey, we just found out that this Sunday we are going to have to move our service to the downstairs theater. This would be a perfect opportunity for you to come early and help out, because it's going to take more volunteers than ever to make sure we have a great experience in the downstairs theater." I took the opportunity to create a sense of urgency—and you know what? New people would sign up to serve. Once they were there, we made sure they enjoyed serving, earnestly thanked them for their time, and asked them to do it again.

When you give potential servers an immediate why, they will often respond. People get involved when they have a specific reason to get involved. Otherwise, they may want to do something, but they can continually justify putting it off until next month, next quarter or next year. Always ask yourself, *What are we doing this week that could get more people involved in serving than last week?* and then challenge new people to serve.

### Renegade Pastor Testimony

Since joining the coaching network with Nelson, I am always excited to get back to my church to share and encourage them with what I've learned from each session. As a result, we're beginning to see person after person rise up and make the commitment to ministry. The coaching hasn't just developed my own leadership, but has also woven its way into everything I'm teaching others. To see others accept the call to ministry is one of the greatest rewards to me as a follower of Christ. How amazing it is to see the ripple effect trickle outward!

Scott Clevenger, Lead Pastor
Christ's Church Camden—Kingsland, Georgia

By challenging your flock in these three areas, you can raise up new givers, engage people in sharing their faith, and connect people to volunteer opportunities. In every instance, you are feeding them. You are discipling them in the ways they need to be discipled in order to grow into fully developing followers of Jesus. What challenge could you present to your church next month? Could you set up a yearlong challenge of some kind? Be creative. Don't let your sheep become too comfortable. Keep stretching them so that they will continue to grow.

## Protect Your Sheep

Protecting your flock may be your greatest responsibility as a shepherd. Do you have processes in place to shield them from the wolves prowling in the hills? How about from the wolves among them dressed in sheep's clothing? You can't hit the cruise button and simply pray that your people will be safe from harm. That's what average pastors do—and they end up with hurt sheep and splintered flocks. Renegades, on the other hand, take intentional steps to protect the flock they've been entrusted to shepherd.

The single best way to protect your people is to set up checkpoints of accountability for those ascending up the ranks of leadership within your church. I've mentioned the membership and growth group covenants we have in place at The Journey. We also have additional covenants that correlate with each new level of responsibility we give someone. For example, there's a covenant for group leaders and another for our team leaders (the high-capacity volunteers directly over our group leaders). These covenants are not unique to the groups system; we have them in place for every level of every ministry within the church. At each successive level, the requirements of the covenant go up. For instance, our group leaders are required to give regularly, but we don't require a tithe. Team leaders, on the other hand, must be tithers in order to continue in the position. If someone can't agree to the advanced requirements, they don't move up the ladder of leadership. That's our way of protecting the flock. Protection comes through accountability.

The single best way to protect your people is to set up checkpoints of accountability for those ascending up the ranks of leadership within your church.

We learned early on to be wary of someone who wants increased responsibility but doesn't want to fulfill the requirements. One of the darkest moments in our church's life together came as a result of not enforcing this level of protection. Many years ago, a charismatic guy I'll call Greg (not his real name) was part of our worship arts team and was quickly progressing to higher and higher levels of responsibility. He had actually made it to a pretty high level of leadership without adhering to the covenant expectations along the way, which was our fault. Once Greg stepped into this relatively significant position of leadership, I started getting a bad vibe from him. He would avoid me after the service; he seemed distant with other leaders; I overheard him talking to people on his team in a questionable way a few times. I started to get uncomfortable.

My first step in response to these signs of trouble was to look into Greg's records. I found an immediate red flag: Greg had never gone through membership class. Next, I pulled his giving history, and found that he actually gave well. (As an aside, whenever I have a question about someone, one of the first things I do is look at his giving record. A person's giving can tell you a lot about how connected his heart is to the church and how mature he is.) I was happy to see Greg's strong giving, but that didn't negate the fact that he had never become a member. So we sat him down and had a conversation with him about the importance of membership class. He made the excuse that he had a commitment to another church and wanted to keep that previous commitment for the time being. He said that if we gave him a little space, he would become a member. So, we let him stay in his position, based on that promise. Bad decision.

A few months later, flying under the radar, Greg moved up to the next level of leadership within worship arts. He became one of 16 team leaders. As such, he directly influenced dozens of other volunteers and had access to a whole database list of people in our church. Again too late, we asked ourselves, "Wait, did Greg ever go through membership class?" He hadn't. (We weren't too quick on the uptake back then.) I bet you can guess where this story is going. Within three months of becoming a team leader, Greg left the church and took 25 people with him. We lost members, committed regular attenders, and people who hadn't even taken the step of salvation yet.

Greg was able to advance to a level that allowed him to cause significant destruction because we failed to hold him accountable to the basic requirements of the covenants we have in place. Consequently, he wasn't on board with the vision and mission of the church, nor was he committed to the requirements of being a member or a team leader. He progressed through the levels of leadership without agreeing to the accompanying expectations—and disaster followed. We can't blame Greg; the responsibility was on our shoulders to protect our other sheep by holding him accountable to certain standards, and we didn't do it.

Accountability leads to protection. You have to decide what you expect of members, volunteers and lay leaders at every level, and then keep people accountable to those expectations. Agreements on the front end prevent disagreements on the back end. By making sure that anyone who is moving up in the church meets the basic requirements you've set for them, you can protect your sheep from being hurt.

 Accountability leads to protection.

While setting up accountability is important for your volunteers and lay leaders, it's even more important for your staff. There are very few things I would fire a staff member over, but hurting the sheep is one of them. The people on my staff are given room to make a lot of mistakes. In fact, I welcome mistakes, as long as someone's not making the same mistake over and over again. But if a staff member hurts the sheep, there's not much leniency. Practically speaking, someone is hurting the sheep when he is not fulfilling his role in relation to the sheep. That is, he's not providing the care he's supposed to, he's not where he's supposed to be when he's supposed to be there to meet with sheep, and/or he's leading his volunteers poorly. You get the idea. Part of your role is to make sure that none of your under-shepherds hurt the sheep. You simply can't allow it to happen.

You have the same call on your life that Peter had on his—to take care of Jesus' sheep. Are you being intentional about it, or are you letting your sheep laze around, get hungry, and wander into danger? I challenge you to start leading, feeding and protecting your sheep like a renegade. Shepherd well the flock God has given you. After all, one day you will present it to the Good Shepherd as the evidence of your work on this earth.

## Renegade Pastor Testimony

I came to a point in my life and ministry where I literally didn't know where to go or what to do. The church was in serious

decline, and I was tired and broken. I didn't want to quit. I wanted to finish well! This is when God led me to Nelson's coaching network. Nelson stretched me out of my comfort zone. Through the coaching, I saw where I needed to grow personally, reignite a passion for reading, and re-engage myself in ministry. I've been learning how to be a shepherd leader, not just a shepherd chaplain. It has changed my life.

Jerry Peterson, Senior Pastor
First Lutheran Church—Oklahoma City, Oklahoma

# *Commitment Six:*
# Maximize Your Church

*Structuring Your Church for Maximum Impact*

It is out of the Word of God that a system
has come to make life sweet.
BENJAMIN HARRISON

Good planning and hard work lead to prosperity,
but hasty shortcuts lead to poverty.
PROVERBS 21:5

What does the full redemptive potential of your church look like? In other words, if everything in your church were operating at the height of capacity and efficiency, how many people would you be reaching with the gospel? How well would you be getting those people plugged into small groups and into serving opportunities? How deeply would you be discipling them in the disciplines essential to their growth? These are serious questions to consider. There are people in your community who won't be reached if your church doesn't reach them. There are people in your church who will never become fully developing followers of Jesus if you don't disciple them well. You are called to cooperate with God in maximizing every area of your church for His glory. The question is: Are you willing to put in the work it takes to do that?

Here's the hard truth: Your church is not currently realizing as much of its potential as it could. There's always more you could do. As a pastor, you live with the constant tension between where your church is and where it could be. All pastors do. Average pastors get comfortable hanging out in the divide between current reality and ultimate potential, reassuring themselves with little white lies like: "We're doing all we can. This is what God has for us." Renegade pastors, on the other hand, use that tension to propel themselves to continually higher levels of influence and impact. They constantly ask questions like: "What can we be doing better? How can we more fully cooperate with God to grow and strengthen this church?"

 **Renegade Commitment Six:** Maximize Your Church

Every church's level of potential is different. Your church's full redemptive potential will not look just like the church down the street or the church the next town over. Reaching your full redemptive potential isn't about hitting a certain number or emulating some other ministry. Be careful not to fall into the comparison trap. Instead, focus with renegade intensity on what God wants to do through the church He has given you. To cooperate with God in positioning your church to have the greatest impact possible, both on the people within it and on the community where you minister, simply make the sixth commitment of a renegade pastor: decide to maximize your church. How? By maximizing the systems that hum beneath its surface.

## Maximized Systems = Maximized Church

Have you ever held a newborn baby? Have you counted tiny fingers and toes or watched a little chest move up and down, drawing breath for the first time? That baby may be a bundle of joy for his parents but, in reality, he's also a bundle of something else. He is a bundle of perfectly formed, intricate systems that are already working together

to keep him alive. Thanks to his tiny circulatory system, his heart is pumping blood through his arteries. Thanks to his respiratory system, his lungs are taking in air. His digestive system is breaking down his mother's milk from the very first drop, and his muscular system is letting him wrap his tiny hand around his father's finger. Even in a brand-new baby, these systems and others are fully developed, fully functioning, and ready to grow with the child as he starts his journey toward adulthood.

God is into systems. He organized the universe with systems. He established the measurement of time through a system. He formed the human body as a cohesive unit of systems. Adam and Eve—unblemished examples of God's craftsmanship—were compilations of the systems that caused them to function. They were perfect adult examples of that newborn baby. Without systems operating under the surface, they would not have been able to walk, talk or even breathe. They wouldn't have been able to experience the pleasures of the garden. Eve wouldn't have been able to pluck the apple from the tree, and Adam wouldn't have been able to take the bite that set God's redemptive plan into motion. Without their systems, they would have remained unmolded lumps of clay, unable to fulfill the purposes of God. From the beginning, God has put systems to work, providing the mechanics and the platform through which He shows His greatness.

One more thing about Adam and Eve: What was the blueprint God used in creating them? Himself. As the Bible affirms, God created man in His own image (see Gen. 1:26-27). Don't miss this: God created beings that function through systems and said they had been made in His own image. Yep, it's safe to say God is into systems.

Paul understood God's affinity for systems. That's why, in trying to help readers wrap their minds around how the church should operate, he compared the Body of Christ to the human body:

> For just as each of us has one body with many members, and these members do not all have the same function, so in

Christ we, though many, form one body, and each member
belongs to all the others (Rom. 12:4-5, *NIV*).

Sounds a lot like how God designed the physical body with
systems, right? Go back and read the verse again, substituting the word
"systems" every time you see the word "members." Makes perfect sense,
doesn't it? And so it is with the church as it is with the human body.
Each system plays an important role. Can the endocrine system say to
the nervous system, "Because I am not the nervous system, I am of no
use"? Of course not. All the parts of the body—both the church body
and the physical body—work together, allowing people to fulfill God's
purposes on this earth. And both of those bodies function best through
well-developed systems.

## The Body Shop

In the 1950s, an American man named Edward Deming transformed
the Japanese automotive industry. Until just after World War II,
few people knew who Deming was. An obscure professor at the
University of Chicago, he spent a lot of time devising and lecturing
on ideas about quality measurement and control. Not long after the
end of the war, leaders in Japan's automotive industry heard about
Deming's research and came to him for advice. They had a notion
that the automobile could be Japan's key to renewed prosperity, but
the industry was currently in shambles. To own a Japanese car was
to own a dud. Something wasn't working right. In the minds of the
industry leaders, that something was their people.

Convinced that their problem was a disinterested, lazy work-
force, the Japanese automotive leaders brought Deming in to
conduct research on how their cars moved from concept to final
product. They wanted to know where the breakdowns were happening and who was responsible. So Deming began a 10-year evaluation.
In the end, his results were surprising. The industry leaders had it
all wrong. They didn't have a people problem at all. In fact, their
employees were committed, hard-working, and eager to put a good

product on the market. They just didn't know how to go about it. Why? Because the industry's systems for moving a car through the stages of production were ineffective. This wasn't a people problem; it was a systems problem.

Deming went to the guys who had hired him and said, "Your systems are giving you exactly what they are designed to give you." In short, he was telling them that they were responsible for their own failures. They had put in place weak systems that, by design, couldn't produce what they wanted. With Deming's help, the industry leaders began working to strengthen their systems and started the turnaround that eventually made Japanese cars the best in the world. To this day, Japan celebrates Deming Day every year, in honor of the man who showed them how to structure for success by maximizing a series of interrelated systems.

## The Power of Systems

You aren't building cars in Japan but, whether you realize it or not, you use systems to help you accomplish your objectives every day. Think about the system you have for getting dressed in the morning. You don't put on your deodorant until you get out of the shower. You drink your coffee before you brush your teeth. Right? There's a way you get ready for the day that makes getting out of the house faster and easier. You also have a system for the way you organize your calendar. You have a system for the way you prepare for the weekend service—even if you don't realize that you do.

 "Your systems are giving you exactly what they are designed to give you." —Edward Deming

I'm on the road a lot, which means I check in and out of hotels regularly. Until recently, I used to leave something behind almost every time I checked out. I would inevitably forget my cell phone, its charger, my keys, or something else I wouldn't think of until I was miles away. So, I developed a simple system. Now, whenever I go into

a hotel room, I put all of my miscellaneous things beside the television, instead of scattering them across the desk, dresser, bedside tables and bathroom vanity. Since I've implemented this system, I don't have to waste time and gas money going back to hotels to pick up the things I've left. I also don't have to deal with the stress of knowing that my phone is going to die any minute or that my house keys are in someone else's hands. This simple system does what a system is meant to do: It saves me stress, time, energy and money.

**S**aves
**Y**ou
**S**tress
**T**ime
**E**nergy
**M**oney

A system is any ongoing process that **S**aves **Y**ou **S**tress, **T**ime, **E**nergy and **M**oney, and continues to produce results. Good systems function under the surface to keep things running smoothly so that you can concentrate on more important priorities. For example, you don't have to think about the fact that your neurological system is allowing you to read and process this information. That system is doing its job, or you wouldn't be able to understand the words in front of you. If you began to see a decline in your cognitive ability—if all of a sudden you couldn't remember or analyze information in the way you always have—you would have to deal with the stress of knowing something was wrong and put a lot of time, energy and money into figuring out where the breakdown was happening. You may not be aware of a system when it is running well, but there is no mistaking when something isn't working like it should.

The same is true in your church. Since the church is a body, it follows that the church also has systems working beneath the surface. I contend that the church is made up of eight systems: (1) the worship planning system, (2) the evangelism system, (3) the assimilation system,

(4) the small-groups system, (5) the ministry system, (6) the steward-ship system, (7) the leadership system, and (8) the strategic system. Each of these systems is present in your church, whether it is healthy and active or not. And just like on Japan's production line, each system is giving you the results it has been designed to give you. If you want to change your results in any area, change the corresponding system in cooperation with the Holy Spirit.

## The Eight Systems of the Church

A few years ago, I became a runner. When I first started running, my cardiovascular system was not very strong. It was there, but it wasn't all that efficient. I could only run for a few minutes at a time before I was spent. But over the course of several months, with directed train-ing, I strengthened my cardiovascular system (not to mention my respiratory and muscular systems), and now I can run long distances without stopping. While I'm proud of my progress, I have a friend who has been running for most of his life and can still run marathons around me. His cardiovascular system is more highly developed than mine because he has put more time and energy into developing it. That's how systems work; if you strengthen them, they grow. While my friend the marathoner and I each have a cardiovascular system, they are in different stages of health based on what we've done to maximize them. See where this is going?

People may look different on the outside, but within every human being is a function of common machinery. Everyone has lungs that circulate air, even though some have bigger, more power-ful lungs than others. Everyone has senses that take in the world, though in some one sense is more elevated than another. In the same way, all churches are made up of the same exact systems, even though those systems may be stronger and more efficient in some churches than in others. The question isn't whether or not these systems are in place, but whether or not they are being exercised, nourished and maximized.

The eight systems of the church are interconnected. None of them can stand alone. And because a church is a living entity, the well-developed systems run whether you are thinking about them or not. Just as you breathe while you sleep, strong systems operate without constant supervision. Still, to make sure all of your church's systems are running correctly, you need to keep a finger on the pulse of each one. If you are disinterested or lazy about growing and maintaining your systems, they won't produce the results you want. They will atrophy from lack of use.

There are simple ways to foster the full potential of your systems—and thereby the full redemptive potential of your church—no matter what stage each one is currently in. Whether your church is like a brand-new baby, just starting the journey of growth, or like a robust adult in the prime of life, its eight systems are in place, waiting to be maximized for life-changing results.

From a health standpoint, there are certain systems you should work on first to reap the fastest results. The key is to do something. Even if you can't overhaul all eight of your systems right away, you can take small immediate action steps within each one that will move your church closer to the vision God has for it. Here's a brief overview of each of the eight church systems, in order of their immediate effectiveness in helping your church reach its full potential, and action steps you can take to start getting each one on track:

## The Assimilation System: Moving People from First-Time Guests to Members

Your Assimilation System is your plan for taking people from their first visit to becoming fully developing members of your church. How do you get people to keep coming back until they are ready to plug in at a deeper level? You can't just expect your first-time guests to return without any intentional action from you and your staff. You have to make sure you are creating environments that make them feel comfortable and welcomed—environments they'll want to re-engage in.

Think about how many first-time guests you have over the course of a year. An average of just 3 guests each week means you influence

more than 150 new people every 12 months. How many of those people are sticking around? To grow consistently, you need to keep 1 in 5 of your first-time guests. There are specific steps you can take to make sure you see that kind of retention. The first step is to be honest about how well your Assimilation System is working right now. Consider these questions:

- When was the last time you looked at your church through a guest's eyes?
- Have you filled out your Connection Card to make sure it is user-friendly?
- What do people say is their first impression of your church?
- How many of your first-time guests end up becoming members? Are you happy with that number?

Implementing good assimilation practices is the fastest way to grow your church. Making small changes in this area can lead to huge growth. (For detailed teaching on the Assimilation System, see my book *Fusion: Turning First-Time Guests into Fully Engaged Members of Your Church*. Also visit www.RenegadePastorBook.com for additional assimilation resources.)

*Immediate Assimilation Action Step*: Handwritten thank-you notes are a powerful assimilation tool, and well worth the effort they require. Start sending a handwritten thank-you note to every first-time guest who visits your church.

## The Stewardship System: Developing Extravagant Givers at Your Church

You will never lead a church of fully developing disciples until you learn to cultivate strong givers. This is where the Stewardship System comes in. How do you encourage people to give for the first time? How do you know when they do? Once they give that first gift, how do you follow up with them? How do you turn sporadic givers into regular givers and teach them the importance of giving the full tithe?

Despite the success we had with The Journey's first giving challenge, most new givers don't go from 0 to 10 percent right away. There is a path you have to lead them down as they mature in their understanding of stewardship. Their growth doesn't happen haphazardly. Having a system in place that allows you to train, educate and nurture extravagant givers is essential to discipling your people in the grace of giving.

So, how effective is your current Stewardship System? Think about these questions:

- Are you modeling extravagant giving?
- When was the last time you taught on the spiritual discipline of giving? (See Chapter 5.)
- Have you put forth a tithe challenge in the last year?

If you will give this system some true attention, you can begin to move the money issue out of the shadows and lead your church into the blessing that comes through honoring God financially. (For detailed teaching on the Stewardship System, see my book *Maximize: How to Develop Extravagant Givers in Your Church*. Also visit www. RenegadePastorBook.com for additional stewardship resources.)

*Immediate Stewardship Action Step*: In the average church, there's about a 30 percent gap between current and potential giving. One simple way you can begin to close that gap is by warning people before you receive the offering. Let them know that the offering bucket will be coming by soon and give them time to prepare their gift. When you catch people off guard, you rob them of the opportunity to give.

## The Evangelism System: Attracting People to Your Church

Have you ever wondered why some churches seem to get all of the new growth while others sit stagnant? Does God just love those pastors more? How does He decide which churches to draw people to? The Principle of Spiritual Readiness teaches that God will never

give you more than you are prepared to handle. You have to do your part to let people know you are in town and ready to receive them.

So, how do you get that message out? How do you invite people to come through your doors for the first time? As you begin to think about your Evangelism System, concentrate on taking advantage of the seasons of the year when people are most willing to come to church for the first time. Keep your culture in mind. Know whether your community will respond best to postcards, emails, phone calls, billboards, or a specific combination of outreach methods. God attracts, but you have to do your part of the preparation.

If you aren't seeing a lot of first-time guests walking through your doors, there's a good chance you aren't maximizing your evangelism efforts. To start revving up this system, consider these questions:

- When was the last time you did a big direct-mail campaign?
- Have you invested in servant evangelism lately? Servant evangelism is simply sharing God's love in practical ways with the people in your community. For a free resource on Servant Evangelism see www.RenegadePastorBook.com.
- Who was the last person you personally invited to church?
- When was the last time you challenged your people to bring friends to a special day?

Evangelism is the cornerstone of everything you do. You'll never be able to cooperate with God in bringing new people into the Kingdom if you can't first bring them through the doors of your church. (For more in-depth information on the Evangelism System, see my book *Ignite: How to Spark Immediate Growth in Your Church*. Also visit www.RenegadePastorBook.com for additional evangelism resources.)

*Immediate Evangelism Action Step*: Think about the next big day coming up at your church. Is Easter approaching? Do you have a new message series kicking off soon? Have some invitation cards printed to correlate with your next big day or new series. Hand those cards out to your people and specifically challenge them to invite three to five friends.

## Renegade Pastor Testimony

I graduated from seminary with just enough information to lead a church of 100. It wasn't until 28 years later that I learned (from Nelson) how the church is made up of different systems. What has transpired since I learned about the systems and began to implement them has changed my ministry. It has taken some time and discipline to completely implement all eight of the systems, but it's worth it. Last Easter, the church had its highest attendance ever at 450. I now know that I can lead a church of not only 100 but of 1,000 because I have systems in place that can keep the church growing and healthy at the same time. Having strong systems has enabled the church to have the financial resources and the volunteers necessary to reach our maximum potential.

Morris Barnett, Senior Pastor
Cliffdale Community Church—Fayetteville, North Carolina

### The Worship Planning System: Planning, Implementing and Evaluating the Weekend Services at Your Church

Sunday is game day. It's the day you need to be at your best; the day you need to be totally reliant on God; and the day you need to have some assurance that things are going to go just like they should so that people will have the best possible opportunity to encounter God. Whether you acknowledge it or not, you already have in place a system for planning, implementing and evaluating your Sunday services. The system may not be giving you the results you want, but it's there.

How do you outline your teaching? How do you coordinate with your worship pastor? If you use message notes, when are they due to the printer? How do you prepare your mind and spirit to preach? How do you debrief with your staff when the services are over? You have a way of doing all of these things, so step back and look at how

efficient your way is. Do you have a system set up that works to your benefit, or do you operate in crisis mode every week?

To start refining your Worship Planning System, make a list of everything that goes into getting ready for the weekend. Think about what you can do to lower your stress and save yourself time, energy and money. As you develop this system, don't forget to evaluate how well things are working in the service each week. Constantly be thinking about how you can improve. After every service, ask yourself and those you trust:

- What was missing?
- What was confusing?
- How can we do things better?

The worst mistake you can make is to let Sunday run on autopilot. God is always up to something new. Make sure you are in a position to magnify whatever that is, week in and week out. (For detailed teaching on creating a strong Worship Planning System, see my book *Engage: A Guide to Creating Life-Transforming Worship Services*.[1] Also visit www.RenegadePastorBook.com for additional worship planning resources.)

*Immediate Worship Planning Action Step*: Do you do a weekly message run-through? If not, I encourage you to start this week. Pull some staff people together on Thursday afternoon and preach the weekend's message to them as if it were Sunday morning. Be open to their feedback and adjust where you need to before the weekend. This one step will improve your preaching exponentially.

## The Ministry System: Mobilizing People for Significant Ministry

The Ministry System, also known as the Volunteer System, determines how you mobilize people for ministry at your church. God created people to serve. If you don't have a system in place to help them get plugged in, you are hurting both yourself and your potential, untapped leaders. At The Journey, our goal is to get 50 percent

of our people involved in serving at least one hour each week. What's your goal? Do you have one? Remember, you can never have too many volunteers. Check up on your Ministry System by considering these questions:

- How many passionate volunteers do you have?
- How many passionate volunteers would you like to have?
- What are you doing to make people want to serve?
- When was the last time you personally took time to invest in your volunteers?

What steps do you need to take to create a volunteer system that makes people want to get involved and do the things you can't hire people to do? Think about what you want your Ministry System to look like one year from today, write that vision down, and get to work. (For detailed teaching on maximizing your Ministry System, see my book *Connect: How to Double Your Number of Volunteers*. Also visit www.RenegadePastorBook.com for additional volunteer recruitment resources.)

*Immediate Ministry Action Step*: This Sunday, put a blank 3x5 notecard in your pocket. As you see new volunteers or people who are doing an exceptional job, write down their names. During the week, shoot those people an email or send a handwritten note to acknowledge and thank them for their service.

## The Small Groups System: Filling and Reproducing Small Groups at Your Church

Believe it or not, it is possible to have 100 percent church participation in small groups. How? By having a strong Small Groups System in place that focuses on this core question: How do we fill and reproduce small groups at our church? Whether you are a church with groups, a church of groups, a church with Sunday School, or a church operating on a semester-based system, you have to have a specific plan in place for filling your current groups and creating new ones.

At The Journey, our Small Groups System is based around four key activities: Focus, Form, Fill and Facilitate. By setting up an ongoing system that focuses, forms, fills and facilitates our groups for success every semester, we see 100 percent participation with low levels of stress, time commitment, expended energy and outgoing money. If you have a weak Small Groups System, you will see problems in many of your other systems as well. By contrast, a strong Small Groups System will help you solve leadership, pastoral care, volunteer and hospitality issues across the board.

Would you say your Small Groups System is healthy? Are you doing your part and seeing God's blessing in this area? Or are you frustrated with sign-ups, participation and results? To take the pulse of this system in your church, think through these questions:

- How many of your regular attenders and members are actively involved in a small group?
- Are you competing against your own groups by offering too many other activities?
- How many passionate group leaders do you have?
- Are you personally involved in a small group? Is everyone on your staff involved in a small group?

Take a hard look at the state of your Small Groups System. Be honest about the level of excitement in your church over groups. Groups are critical to the continued growth of your people. (For more on building a Small Groups System that results in 100 percent participation, see my book *Activate: An Entirely New Approach to Small Groups*.[2] Also visit www.RenegadePastorBook.com for additional small-group resources.)

*Immediate Small Groups Action Step:* If you aren't in a small group, join one today. Also, require everyone on your staff to be actively involved in a small group. Your people won't engage in what you aren't modeling.

## The Leadership System: Developing Leaders at All Levels of Your Church

As your church grows, you will need to develop staff, lay leaders and high-level volunteers. What kind of plan do you have in place to make sure you are developing people in the right way? What tools are you using? How do you determine the qualifications of a leader? A healthy Leadership System will help you with staff management, organizational efficiency and personal development. To evaluate your current Leadership System, consider these questions:

- When was the last time you invested in developing new leaders?
- How are you helping your current leaders grow personally and spiritually?
- Are you modeling the kind of leadership you want to see from others?
- Are any of your levels of leadership in need of more people?

To start structuring this system for health, define the expectations of every leadership position in your church. Assign covenant requirements for each role, and make sure you don't let anyone blindly climb the leadership ladder (as discussed in Chapter 5). Put deadlines on service roles so that everyone who agrees to serve in a high-level volunteer position knows that it isn't forever. Take a hard look at who is moving up through the ranks, and make sure you have enough leaders at all levels of service. Don't forget to make the connections between systems—the Ministry System is a direct inroad to the Leadership System. Everything works together for optimal success. (For additional resources on the Leadership System, visit www.RenegadePastorBook.com.)

*Immediate Leadership Action Step:* Find a good book on leadership and have your staff read it together. Plan a time to discuss the application points. (For leadership book recommendations, go to www.RenegadePastorBook.com.)

## The Strategic System: Constantly Evaluating and Improving Your Church

The Strategic System sits above the other seven systems and serves as the overarching evaluation tool that ties them all together. By making sure you are continually evaluating and refining all of your other systems, the Strategic System gives you the opportunity and the ability to stay on the road toward constant improvement, rather than slipping toward average. A well thought-out strategy will help you become more faithful and fruitful in every area of your ministry. To gauge the health of your Strategic System, consider these questions:

- When was the last time you checked in with your eight church systems?
- How prepared are you for what God wants to do in and through your church?
- Do your staff members know and understand your church's strategy?

Think of the Strategic System as your church's annual physical. Just as with your body, if you don't pay periodic attention to how the systems are working, disease can creep in. The Strategic System keeps your church humming along efficiently and ensures that you are always proactively looking for ways to improve. As you sow some time and effort into your Strategic System, you will reap rewards in your other seven systems. Don't skimp on strategy. It's the thread that ties your church systems together. (For additional resources on the Strategic System, visit www.RenegadePastorBook.com.)

*Immediate Strategic Action Step:* Block off some time in your calendar for reviewing your Strategic System. Meet with key staff members to discuss how you can improve your church's overall strategy.

## The Relationship Factor

No matter how strong your eight systems are, they can never be fully maximized until you have the right people around you. Relationships are the tracks on which successful systems run. Take a look at this diagram:

The best results come from having good people working within good systems. As Deming found in Japan, good people working in bad systems can lead to a lot of frustration and misunderstanding. Have you been there? Maybe some of the people problems you've experienced haven't really been people problems at all. Then again, maybe you have well-developed systems in place, but some of the wrong people working in them. If that's the case, you've probably been seeing better than average results, but you can't quite break through to the next level. Systems will never be enough on their own. The people inside have to be motivated to work together in pursuit of a common vision—in this case, the vision to give people the best possible opportunity to become fully developing followers of Jesus.

God wired the planets to operate through systematic patterns. He created the soil to produce through strategic systems of sowing

and reaping. He wired human beings to function with certain cycles and according to certain timetables. Following the trends God has put in place is the best way to reach this world with His glory. If you look at the way He set things up, and then align yourself and your ministry accordingly, you can start every day with the assurance that you are doing His will.

God wants to work in your church. He wants more for your church body than you can even dream. Make sure you do your part to maximize these eight systems fully so that God can work through them mightily. (For free online training on each of the eight systems of a healthy church, visit www.RenegadePastorBook.com.)

### Renegade Pastor Testimony

My acquaintance with Nelson and the Renegade Pastors Network began at a live event a few years ago. I went with several other pastors from the community, but came away with a singular life-changing experience. The systems concept Nelson shared was the missing piece in my ministry. As I learned about healthy church systems and how to implement them in my ministry, my stress level dropped, joy in ministry returned, and my personal walk with God became even closer. And the church . . . well, it went from being in a death spiral to over a 100 percent increase in attendance at every weekly worship service and to being financially blessed—but that's not even the greatest thing. What really mattered was the community impact that the congregation grew to have for the Lord. The systems work when you invite God to work the systems with you!

Carl Barnhardt, Lead Pastor
The Pointe—Leesburg, Georgia

# *Commitment Seven:*
# Expand God's Kingdom

*Embracing Your Place Within the Bigger Picture*

Expect great things from God; attempt great things for God.
WILLIAM CAREY

Your kingdom come, your will be done, on earth as it is in heaven.
JESUS (MATTHEW 6:10, *NIV*)

You and your church are just one thread of the grand tapestry God is weaving together to draw people to Himself and reveal His glory to the world. Not only does He expect you to do all you can to make your own thread strong and vibrant, but He also wants you to be aware of the specific ways He is calling you to enhance the overall masterpiece. While becoming a renegade pastor hinges on making the personal commitments necessary to take your life and church to the next level, it also requires that you keep an eye toward the larger work God is unfolding all around you—the work He is doing in your community, in your city, in your state, in the country and across the world.

The seventh commitment of being a renegade pastor—Expand God's Kingdom—is a subtle, natural outgrowth of the fifth and sixth commitments (discussed in the last two chapters). I contend that the most important thing you can do to effectively expand God's

kingdom is to shepherd your flock well and maximize the church God has entrusted to you. Healthy, vibrant local churches are God's greatest tool for evangelizing and discipling the world. When each individual church is actively engaged in reaching its full redemptive potential, the resulting synergy among them strengthens and grows God's overall kingdom. So as you make this final commitment of being a renegade pastor, you underscore your decision to partner with God in abandoning average thinking and the average results that follow. That said, the seventh commitment also shines a light toward the opportunities you have to engage in God's work on a larger scale.

**Renegade Commitment Seven:** Expand God's Kingdom

## Embracing a Bifocal Vision

There's a distinct difference in how average pastors and renegade pastors view the expansion of God's kingdom. Average pastors wrestle with one of two opposing temptations. Either they are tempted to focus solely on their own churches, to the exclusion of any involvement in the greater Kingdom, or they get so excited about outside kingdom opportunities that they let their own churches plateau and fail. Over the years, I have worked with a number of pastors who have fallen into both of these traps.

Renegade pastors, on the other hand, have bifocal vision. They primarily keep their eyes on what is going on in their own churches, but they are also mindful of their responsibility to the bigger picture. If you've ever put on a pair of bifocal glasses, you know that bifocal vision isn't an equal 50/50 split of attention; it's more like 95/5. About 95 percent of the lens allows you to focus where 95 percent of your attention needs to be. The other 5 percent of the lens comes into play less frequently, but it is still an important element of your overall vision.

As you think about expanding God's kingdom, that's how your attention should be divided. Ninety-five percent of your energy

should be focused on building up the church you are called to, and 5 percent should be given to engaging in larger-scale ministry opportunities outside your doors. Through the pages of this book, you've discovered how to transform your life and church from average to renegade, thereby fully cooperating with God to make your primary ministry all it can be. In closing, I challenge you to think beyond your church's operation and ask God how He would have you engage in the work of expanding His overall Kingdom.

When it comes to moving beyond your immediate ministry concerns and into the realm of the greater Kingdom, there are countless approaches. You can do missions work locally or overseas; get involved with community service or school boards in your area; invest time with orphans, widows and the needy; or do any number of other things. You will have to figure out what your 5 percent focus should be directed toward. That said, here are three ways I would encourage you to get involved in the bigger picture: through (1) launching new churches, (2) raising up new leaders, and (3) investing in the other pastors around you.

## Launching New Churches

Too many growing churches ask themselves the wrong question. They ask, "Is it God's will for us to grow larger or for us to plant other churches?" It's not an either/or proposition. Having a hand in church planting is a powerful way to engage with God in growing the Kingdom. Thanks to bifocal vision, God can fully intend for you to do both. But first your own church needs to be on a healthy trajectory. Don't be overly eager to start new churches too soon. Just as a 10-year-old child is not ready to become a parent, a church that is still dependent on outside support, has weak systems, or isn't flourishing itself is not mature enough to start new, healthy churches.

Once your church is strong, or at least moving solidly in the right direction, you can look through your bifocals and ask God what part He would have you take in starting new churches. As I've mentioned, churches are God's greatest tool for evangelism and

discipleship. If you can help start more, by all means do. When you feel like your church is ready to make the leap, commit to launching new congregations as quickly and healthily as possible. As a model for where to launch a new church, look to the guidelines Jesus Himself laid out:

> But you will receive power when the Holy Spirit comes upon you. And you will be my witnesses, telling people about me everywhere—in Jerusalem, throughout Judea, in Samaria, and to the ends of the earth (Acts 1:8).

According to Jesus, you should have an eye toward starting new churches locally (Jerusalem), regionally (Judea), nationally/cross-culturally (Samaria), and globally (to the ends of the earth). If you feel God calling you to start a church in any of these areas, prayerfully lay out a three- to five-year game plan and surrender it to Him. (To learn more about launching new, healthy churches, see my free church-planting resources at www.RenegadePastorBook.com and my book *Launch: Starting a New Church from Scratch*.[1])

## Raising Up New Leaders

What are you doing to identify and encourage people in your church who may feel God calling them to ministry? How would you help someone who is being led to be a pastor move forward? This is one area where the church has dropped the ball in recent decades. Think about it. When was the last time you heard someone preach on the call to ministry? Or even teach a sliver of a message on the topic? When was the last time you personally invited people in your church to answer the call to ministry? To say that the church's traditional emphasis on helping young leaders discern a potential call and then setting them on the right path has dwindled is an understatement. It's time for a fresh mindset and a new imperative when it comes to challenging and equipping new leaders to do God's work.

Part of your role in shepherding your flock well is to connect your people in service, as discussed in Chapter 5. At the most supreme level possible, that means raising up those leaders who are called into full-time ministry work. Think of the call to ministry as the highest level of service your people can attain. It's not a level they can aspire to based on their own will, but rather one that God has to invite them to. If you see people eagerly scaling the levels of lay leadership in your church, especially young people, don't shy away from introducing a conversation about the call to ministry and helping them articulate the prompting they may be feeling deep down. If you aren't walking in awareness of how you can help the budding ministers or missionaries around you, you'll do both them and the Kingdom a disservice. On the other hand, as you are open to raising them up, you will be taking an active role in expanding God's work beyond your doors.

At The Journey, we have been fortunate to see more than a dozen men and women called out of our congregation and into full-time ministry. These individuals are now scattered around the globe, working in various churches or parachurch organizations. While I'm thankful that God used The Journey as part of His plan for the lives of these young (and a few not so young) servants, I often wonder if the number should actually be much higher. I have to confess that I haven't always done everything I could to raise awareness about the call to ministry. Now, I am constantly reminding myself to be on the lookout for the one, two or three people among our volunteers whom God might be planning to raise up to be pastors on our staff, or who may be called to lead new churches or to pastor existing churches in need.

My challenge to you—and to myself—is this: As you lead and equip your church, be diligent about raising up leaders in various levels of service; and as you do, don't forget to cooperate with God in calling out those who are truly called for the sake of Christ and the expansion of the Kingdom. (For a list of resources on the call to ministry, visit www.RenegadePastorBook.com.)

## Investing in Other Pastors

In the business world, many leaders have a problem complimenting and investing in one another because they live with a scarcity mentality. Unfortunately, this mentality has become too common among pastors, as well. I see it all the time. Take a look at how Steven Covey defines the issue in *The 7 Habits of Highly Effective People*:

> Most people are deeply scripted in what I call the Scarcity Mentality. They see life as having only so much, as though there were only one pie out there. And if someone were to get a big piece of the pie, it would mean less for everybody else. . . .
>
> People with a Scarcity Mentality have a very difficult time sharing recognition and credit, power or profit—even with those who help in the production. They also have a very hard time being genuinely happy for the successes of other people—even, and sometimes especially, members of their own family or close friends and associates. . . .
>
> Although they might verbally express happiness for others' success, inwardly they are eating their hearts out. Their sense

of worth comes from being compared, and someone else's success, to some degree, means their failure. . . .

They're always comparing, always competing. . . . It's difficult for people with a Scarcity Mentality to be members of a complementary team. They look on differences as signs of insubordination and disloyalty.

The Abundance Mentality, on the other hand, flows out of a deep inner sense of personal worth and security. It is the paradigm that there is plenty out there and enough to spare for everybody. It results in sharing. . . . It opens possibilities, options, alternatives, and creativity. . . . A character rich in integrity, maturity, and the Abundance Mentality has a genuineness that goes far beyond technique, or lack of it, in human interaction.[2]

You are not in competition with the other pastors in your area or in your denomination. You are on the same team with them. Your competition—and theirs—is everything that distracts people in your community from attending church and growing in their faith. You compete with the bars, restaurants and events that keep people out late on Saturday night. You compete with the clubs that lead your people to enter into unhealthy relationships. You compete with lake houses and weekend beach trips. You compete with NFL pre-game shows and early kick-offs during football season. But you do not compete against the other pastors around you who are trying to maximize their churches and disciple people into being fully developing followers of Jesus. They are your teammates; decide to treat them as such.

 You are not in competition with the other pastors in your area or in your denomination.

The Principle of Learn and Return is one of my all-time favorite principles. The idea behind it is that when you come across something that benefits the work of the Kingdom, you share it. When you

learn something, you pass the knowledge along to the other leaders around you. It's impossible to practice the Principle of Learn and Return if you are operating out of a scarcity mentality—if you are always afraid that somebody else's church is going to draw a bigger crowd, be better thought of in the community, or be more effective at discipling people. But when you embrace the abundance mentality, as Covey suggests, and realize that sharing with and building up your fellow pastors benefits not only your community but also the overall Kingdom, then you will reap the ultimate benefit too. After all, a rising tide raises all ships.

When you come across something that works in your church, tell someone else about it. Invest in the pastors and other leaders God has put in your vicinity. As you do, He may even lead you to learn and return on a higher level. What begins as local, word-of-mouth sharing could eventually become knowledge that's so significant you need to package it and make it available to pastors around the country or even around the world. That's exactly what happened to me. As God has blessed The Journey with unique growth in large, unchurched areas of the country and given me insight into tools and strategies that can work for pastors anywhere, I have made a commitment to return what I've learned through my organization, Church Leader Insights (www.ChurchLeaderInsights.com). As you learn—either through my resources, through the resources of others, and/or through your own experiences—I invite you to return the knowledge to the Kingdom by telling others. Here are a few practical tips for learning and returning:

- Share this book and other books that are having an impact on you with the pastors you know. Set up a time to talk through the most applicable principles.
- As you begin working on and learning to maximize the systems in your church, tell other pastors what's working for you and encourage them to begin focusing on their systems as well. Direct them to the free e-book *Healthy Systems, Healthy Church* at www.RenegadePastorBook.com.

- As you discover audio resources and seminars that are helpful to you, share them with pastors in your area.
- When God teaches you something powerful about leading His church, don't keep it to yourself. Return it to the Kingdom by telling others.

Discovering exactly how God wants to direct your bifocal vision will be a process of prayer and seeking, but the three opportunities mentioned here—launching new churches, raising up new leaders, and investing in other pastors—are powerful places to begin. As you commit to ensuring that your own life and ministry reflect God's excellence, with an eye toward enhancing God's overall work in the ways you are led, you will truly be expanding His kingdom on this earth as it is in heaven.

## Renegade Pastor Testimony

I had been pastoring two rural Wisconsin churches for a number of years and had experienced some great revitalization and growth, when I realized that I had no idea what to do next. I was at the limit of my know-how. I had staff and leadership looking to me for direction and, although I knew the vision for what needed to happen, I had no idea how to go about achieving it. That's when I signed up for coaching with Nelson. The coaching process gave me guidelines not just about how to do the work of the church, but also about how to think about doing the work of the church. Over the past three years, our church has grown substantially in attendance, depth of faith, excitement and stewardship. The key to all of that has been my growth as a leader, pastor, follower and family man. It's true that growth happens in coaching. From my own growth through coaching, I have had opportunities to lead and teach, not only in the churches of BMZ, but with numerous other pastors in the state of Wisconsin.

As I have been blessed by Nelson's coaching, I am trying
to bless others for the sake of the Church. I had no idea
I would go beyond leading/pastoring a local church. I am
blessed, humbled and privileged to have a chance to teach
others to lead.

Stan Pegram, Lead Pastor
BMZ Church—Boscobel, Wisconsin

## A Network of Renegades

Let me ask you again: Why did you go into ministry in the first
place? Did you become a pastor because you wanted to do average things with average people for an average God? If you are still
reading this book, you have proven that the answer is no. You want
more than average. You have a vision of the excellence God is calling
you to, and you want to embrace it. You want to stand alongside
the great renegade leaders throughout history and do your part to
cooperate with God in reaching the world for His glory. Your life is
about more than going through the routine of run-of-the-mill days.
You understand the importance of overcoming the pull of resistance
and creating a strong, godly life and legacy.

If you have decided to make each of the seven commitments
of a renegade pastor, congratulations! You are well on your way to
embracing the ultimate call God has put on your life. Still, there's
a trap waiting for you if you aren't careful. While you can begin
moving toward a renewed life and ministry with what you've learned
here, going renegade is an endeavor that can't be effectively tackled
alone. You need accountability. In order to make and keep these
commitments, you need to be around like-minded people—to link
arms with other passionate pastors who want to leave average in the
dust. As King Solomon writes:

Two people are better off than one, for they can help each
other succeed. If one person falls, the other can reach out

and help. But someone who falls alone is in real trouble. Likewise, two people lying close together can keep each other warm. But how can one be warm alone? A person standing alone can be attacked and defeated, but two can stand back-to-back and conquer. Three are even better, for a triple-braided cord is not easily broken (Eccles. 4:9-12).

When you make the decision to go renegade, the enemy will do all he can to trip you up and keep you mired in a life of mediocrity. He doesn't want you to abandon average. He hates the thought of you living out God's vision for your life and for your church. With the support and encouragement of other leaders on the same journey, you will be better able to thwart his attacks and stay passionately engaged in accomplishing the renegade vision God has given you.

But you still need one more thing—a coach. The power of a coach who has done, and is still doing, what you want to do cannot be overstated. As discussed in Chapter 3, nothing can better equip you for the mission you've been given than to submit yourself to a coach who understands the call God has put on your life and can help you fulfill your potential. My calling in life is to equip pastors like you—pastors who demand godly excellence in both life and ministry; pastors who aren't content with average. To that end, I have created a private pastors network for you and other leaders who think like you do—leaders who expect great things from God and are willing to attempt great things for God. If the principles and truths contained in these pages have resonated with you, then I personally invite you to solidify your renegade intentions by joining the Renegade Pastors Network.

The Renegade Pastors Network is an exclusive, monthly, private network. Picking up where the material in this book leaves off, it will help you achieve personal growth, find ministry/life balance, and accomplish the full vision God has given you for your work in His kingdom. Think of it as a team environment, complete with other strong players who will pull you up to your highest level of potential,

and led by an experienced coach who is in the trenches every day, living the renegade life right alongside you. Your membership in the Renegade Pastors Network will include:

- A private, live, monthly update and strategic leadership briefing with me.
- Monthly equipping interview calls with other like-minded leaders and authors.
- Private call-in hours during which you and I can talk specifically about your church and ministry.
- Access to the membership website, blog and resources.
- Access to Renegade Pastors resource documents and a comprehensive directory.
- A significant discount on all Church Leader Insights resources.
- Private invitations to, and free attendance at, the annual Renegade Pastors Conferences.
- Lowest registration cost for all Church Leader Insights events and webinars.
- Plus much more.

The information I've been able to cover in these pages is just the tip of the iceberg. More details, insight and tools for abandoning average wait just beneath the surface. If you are willing, I would love to partner with you in discovering the depths of what the renegade life entails. I can help you take specific steps to challenge status quo thinking and be obedient to God, even as you rebel against resistance. I will stand beside you as you show the watching world what it looks like to be contrarian for Kingdom purposes on a daily basis and live passionately abandoned to the plans of God. If you are ready, you can walk away from mediocrity and frustration once and for all. You can finally find true fulfillment as you fully embrace the call God has put on your life. I will be right there with you every step of the way. (For more detailed information on joining the

Renegade Pastors Network, along with a list of all the bonuses for immediate action, go to www.RenegadePastorBook.com.)

Remember, the commitments you choose to make determine the direction of your life. Deciding to embrace the seven commitments of a renegade pastor sets you apart from the crowd, proving that you are ready to take your place alongside the great renegade leaders who have come before you. As you move down the path of renegade living, I will be praying for you every step of the way. I will be praying for your church and for the increased redemptive potential you are going to begin seeing. I will be praying for your family—for the bonds that are going to be strengthened and the legacy that you are now going to be creating. I will be praying for you as you face resistance day in and day out—as you will—and choose to shake off its pull and run with abandon toward the plans God has for you.

Welcome to this new journey. Welcome to the peace that comes with knowing you are partnering fully with God to be the person and the pastor you were created to be. Welcome to the renegade life.

Now all glory to God, who is able, through his mighty power at work within us, to accomplish infinitely more than we might ask or think. Glory to him in the church and in Christ Jesus through all generations forever and ever! Amen (Eph. 3:20-21).

# *Postscript*

I hope this book will become a conversation starter between us. I am constantly developing resources and gathering ideas to help you abandon average and fully live the Renegade Pastor lifestyle. Let's stay in touch, either indirectly through your subscription to my free newsletter or directly as you officially join the Renegade Pastors Network. Find out about both at this book's website:

**www.RenegadePastorBook.com**

You can also use the website to connect with me. I would love to hear your story, and to continue discussing the ways we can grow together for God's glory.

Your partner in ministry,

Nelson Searcy
Lead Pastor, The Journey Church
Lead Renegade Pastor, www.RenegadePastors.com

# The Seven Commitments Scripture Guide

No book, regardless of its length, is ever complete. This one is no different. My passion for teaching on the renegade commitments knows no end, but word count requirements demand that I make sacrifices in terms of what I can and should include. To partially make up for this dilemma, I present you with the self-study guide below. These selected Scriptures will allow you to dig deeper into each of the seven Renegade Pastor Commitments. This guide, too, is incomplete, but it should at least provide some sturdy guideposts for additional study.

## Commitment One: Follow Your Lord
Doing the Work of God Without
Destroying God's Work in You
Matthew 6:33; Matthew 10:38-39; Mark 8:34; Luke 9:23-24; John 3:16; John 8:12; John 10:4-5; John 10:27-28; Romans 6:23; Philippians 1:21-24; Philippians 3:8-9; Hebrews 12:1-2; James 1:22; Revelation 3:16

## Commitment Two: Love Your Family
Refusing to Sacrifice Your Family on the Altar of Ministry
Genesis 2:23-24; Psalm 127:3; Matthew 19:4-6; Mark 10:5-9; 1 Corinthians 7:3-4; Ephesians 5:25-33; Ephesians 6:1-4; Colossians 3:19-21; Hebrews 13:4; 1 Timothy 1:5; 1 Timothy 3:5; 1 Peter 3:7

### Commitment Three: Fulfill Your Calling
Becoming All God Has Called You to Be
Isaiah 6:7-8; Ephesians 4:11-12; 1 Timothy 3:1-7;
1 Timothy 5:1; Titus 1:6-9; James 3:1; 1 Peter 5:1-4

### Commitment Four: Manage Your Time
Taking Control of Your Most Limited Commodity
Psalm 39:4-5; Psalm 90:4,10,12; Proverbs 6:6-8;
Ecclesiastes 3:1-8; Luke 14:28; John 9:4; Romans 13:11;
Ephesians 5:15-17; Colossians 4:5; James 4:14

### Commitment Five: Shepherd Your Flock
Demystifying Your Job Description
Proverbs 27:23; Jeremiah 3:15; John 13:34-35; John
21:15-17; Acts 20:28; Romans 12:8; Ephesians 4:12;
1 Timothy 3:1-7; Titus 1:6-9; Hebrews 13:17; 1 Peter 5:2-4

### Commitment Six: Maximize Your Church
Structuring Your Church for Maximum Impact
1 Chronicles 12:32; Proverbs 11:14; Proverbs 27:23;
Matthew 10:16; Matthew 16:18; Luke 14:28; John 12:32;
Acts 2:42-47; Acts 6:1-3; Romans 12:2,8; 1 Corinthians
3:7-8,11; Ephesians 4:11-12; 1 Timothy 4:13; Titus 1:5;
James 1:5

### Commitment Seven: Expand God's Kingdom
Embracing Your Place Within the Bigger Picture
Genesis 12:1-3; Isaiah 6:8; Matthew 9:37-38; Matthew
13:18-23; Matthew 16:19; Matthew 22:9-10; Matthew
24:14; Matthew 28:18-20; Luke 10:2; John 14:11-12;
John 15:8,16; John 17:15; John 20:21; Acts 1:8; Acts
10:42-43; Romans 10:15; Ephesians 3:7-8; 2 Timothy 4:5

# *Endnotes*

## Introduction—Abandoning Average: A Tale of Two Pastors

1. Steven Pressfield, *Do the Work!: Overcome Resistance and Get out of Your Own Way* (Hastings, NY: Do You Zoom, 2011), pp. 6,8-9.
2. R. A Nack, *Work-in-Text for Earl Nightingale's Lead the Field* (Chicago: Nightingale-Conant, 1974).

## Chapter 2—Commitment Two: Love Your Family

1. Robert Clinton, "Finishing Well," *Clinton Biblical Leadership Commentary CD*, 1999. http://garyrohrmayer.typepad.com/files/3finishwell articles.pdf.
2. Nelson Searcy with Jennifer Dykes Henson, *The Generosity Ladder: Your Next Step to Financial Peace* (Grand Rapids, MI: Baker Books, 2010).
3. Dave Ramsey, *Dave Ramsey's Complete Guide to Money* (Brentwood, TN: Lampo Press, 2012).
4. Jerry B. Jenkins, *Hedges: Loving Your Marriage Enough to Protect It* (Wheaton, IL: Crossway Books, 2005).

## Chapter 3—Commitment Three: Fulfill Your Calling

1. Nelson Searcy with Jennifer Dykes Henson, *Fusion: Turning First-Time Guests into Fully Engaged Members of Your Church* (Ventura, CA: Regal Books, 2007).

## Chapter 4—Commitment Four: Manage Your Time

1. H. Jackson Brown, *Life's Little Instruction Book: Simple Wisdom and a Little Humor for Living a Happy and Rewarding Life* (Nashville, TN: Thomas Nelson, 2012), p. 95.
2. Brian Tracy, *Eat That Frog!: 21 Great Ways to Stop Procrastinating and Get More Done in Less Time* (San Francisco: Berrett-Koehler, 2001), pp. 2-3.
3. C. H. Spurgeon, *The Preacher's Power and the Conditions of Obtaining It: The Sword and the Trowel* (Liskeard, Cornwall, UK: Diggory Press, 2007).

## Chapter 5—Commitment Five: Shepherd Your Flock

1. Nelson Searcy with Jennifer Dykes Henson, *Maximize: How to Develop Extravagant Givers in Your Church* (Grand Rapids, MI: Baker Books, 2010).
2. Nelson Searcy with Jennifer Dykes Henson, *Ignite: How to Spark Immediate Growth in Your Church* (Grand Rapids, MI: Baker Books, 2009).
3. Nelson Searcy with Jennifer Dykes Henson, *Connect: How to Double Your Number of Volunteers* (Grand Rapids, MI: Baker Books, 2012).

## Chapter 6—Commitment Six: Maximize Your Church

1. Nelson Searcy and Jason Hatley, with Jennifer Dykes Henson, *Engage: A Guide to Creating Life-Transforming Worship Services* (Grand Rapids, MI: Baker Books, 2011).
2. Nelson Searcy and Kerrick Thomas, *Activate: An Entirely New Approach to Small Groups* (Ventura, CA: Regal Books, 2008).

## Chapter 7—Commitment Seven: Expand God's Kingdom

1. Nelson Searcy and Kerrick Thomas, *Launch: Starting a New Church from Scratch* (Ventura, CA: Regal Books, 2006).
2. Stephen Covey, *The 7 Habits of Highly Effective People* (London: Simon & Schuster, 1999), pp. 219-220.

## Join the Renegade Pastors Network NOW for half off your first month (only $49) and get $813.20 in FREE RESOURCES!

The Renegade Pastors Network is about a comprehensive approach to life and ministry. As a member, each month Nelson Searcy will help you stay one step ahead of the calendar, make the most of your time and resources, and fulfill your calling for the sake of the Kingdom.

### As soon as you join, you'll receive the following FREE resources:

- Improve the Financial Fitness of Your Church ($99.95 value)
- The Strategy Seminar ($99.95 value)
- From Stress to Rest sermon series ($99.95 value)
- Forgiveness: The Real F Word sermon series ($99.95 value)
- Relationship Rescue sermon series ($99.95 value)
- Introduction to Church Systems webinar ($49.95 value)
- Improve the Financial Fitness of Your Church webinar ($49.95 value)
- Managing the Stress of Ministry ($29.95 value)
- Debt-Free Pastor ($29.95 value)
- Fasting For Spiritual Breakthrough ($29.95 value)
- Maximizing Summer E-book ($23.95 value)
- The Thursday Midnight Rule ($19.95 value)
- What Gets Measured ($19.95 value)
- Personal Growth Tips ($19.95 value)
- The Power of a Combined Service ($19.95 value)
- The Decision Dilemma ($19.95 value)

*Your monthly membership in the NEW Renegade Pastors Network will help you achieve personal growth, ministry-life balance and accomplish great things for God's Kingdom.*

### But the network is far more than just the resources you receive. The focus this network provides for your ministry and the ideas and insights in your life are simply priceless.

**Sign up today for half off (just $49 for the first month) and receive your $813.20 in FREE bonus resources now:**

## www.RenegadePastorBook.com